YOUR LIFE'S WORK IS *YOU!*
NOW YOU CAN MAKE
YOUR LIFE WORK!

"What I'm doing in my book is sharing my experience of the training, the seminar programs, and the est organization; re-creating that experience as it happened. . . .

The training made it possible for me to take all the things I had known as intellectual concepts and bright ideas and have them become experiences for me so that they became *real* in my life. . . .

est was like a laser; it took all the light in the rainbow and condensed it into a single beam."

Now you can get on that beam—and be more alive—through est!

est:
MAKING LIFE WORK

est:
Making Life Work

ROBERT A. HARGROVE

A DELL BOOK

Published by
DELL PUBLISHING CO., INC.
1 Dag Hammarskjold Plaza
New York, N.Y. 10017

ACKNOWLEDGMENTS

Excerpt from *Be Here Now* by Ram Das: © Lama Foundation 1971. Used by permission.

"Taking the Mystery Out of Mastery" by Werner Erhard: Reprinted with the permission of Spiritual Community Publications from *A Pilgrim's Guide to Planet Earth*, copyright © 1974 by Spiritual Community, Box 1080, San Rafael, Ca. 94902.

Interview with Robert Hargrove and excerpts from interview with Werner Erhard: Reprinted by permission from *East West Journal*. Copyright 1975, 1974 by *East West Journal*, 29 Farnsworth Street, Boston, Ma. 02210.

Excerpt from *Unfinished Animal* by Theodore Roszak: Used by permission of Harper & Row, Publishers, Inc.

Excerpt from *Zen and Japanese Culture* by Daisetz T. Suzuki: Bollingen Series LXIX (copyright © 1959 by Bollingen Foundation), reprinted by permission of Princeton University Press.

Excerpt from *The Electric Kool-Aid Acid Test* by Tom Wolfe: Reprinted with the permission of Farrar, Straus & Giroux, Inc. Copyright © 1968 by Tom Wolfe, copyright © 1967 by the World Journal Tribune Corporation. Used by permission of Weidenfeld and Nicolson Ltd.

Copyright © 1976 by Robert A. Hargrove.

All rights reserved.
No part of this book may be reproduced in any form
without the prior written permission of the Publisher,
excepting brief quotes used in connection with reviews
written specifically for inclusion
in a magazine or newspaper.
Dell ® 681510, Dell Publishing Co., Inc.
Reprinted by arrangement with Delacorte Press.
Printed in the United States of America.

First Dell Printing—June 1976

*Dedicated to my parents
Howard and Beatrice Hargrove
and to their parents
and to my children*

CONTENTS

	Introduction	11
I.	Nothing Like You've Ever Seen	17
II.	Miracles and Realizations	25
III.	When You Know That You Don't Know	39
IV.	What You Resist, Persists	62
V.	Out There in the Illusion	80
VI.	Successive Moments of Now	104
VII.	The Mastery of Life	124
	i. *Be Here Now*	138
	ii. *What's So*	144
	iii. *About Sex*	150
	iv. *Self-Expression*	154
	v. *The Body*	158
	vi. *est and Life*	164
VIII.	The Wizard of *est*	174
IX.	"I Am Moved by Your Support"	212
	Epilogue	236
	Acknowledgments	238

Author's Note

When one comes from his experience, everything he says is perfect; it's just a matter of being accurate. There are no accuracies or inaccuracies in this book; there is only what I "got."

Because my experience may differ from someone else's, and out of respect to the privacy of the individuals concerned, I have changed the names of certain persons whenever it has been appropriate. This includes all the people who stood up and shared themselves in the training and seminar program. It also includes the names of the trainers.

One creates from nothing. As for how it all began, it never did.

INTRODUCTION

This introduction is based on an interview with the author that appeared in the EAST WEST JOURNAL, December 1975. The author was editor/publisher of the EWJ from 1972 to 1974. The original version has been edited by the author.

EWJ: Could you give us a brief history of your association with est—when you first heard about it, when you decided to do the training?
RH: I first heard about est when I was editor of the *East West Journal*. Fred Rohe, who wrote a book called *The Zen of Running*, asked me if we wanted to run an interview of Werner Erhard, and I said, "OK, send it in. I'll see what it looks like." When the interview came in, it was about thirty pages long and I was reluctant to read it. I let it sit in my drawer for about a week. Then I picked it up and started reading it; about midway into the second paragraph I started reading it aloud, and I called about three other people into my office to have them hear it, because there was something about it that I could really connect with. It wasn't so much what Erhard was saying in the interview, and it wasn't so much that he was one of the superstars in the spiritual

supermarket—because from my position as editor of the *EWJ*, I had talked to just about everyone who was anyone on that scene. There was something about him ... well, at the end of the interview, I said, "This is a person whom it's possible for me to be friends with," and I felt a very direct friendship and connection with him from that point on. I didn't have any compulsion to take the training—it was just one of the things that came through the office.

When some of the staff left the *East West Journal* to start the *New Age Journal*, we developed problems in communication, and I decided that it might be a good idea if the group as a whole took est to develop a language and a common basis of experience through which we could really communicate to each other and get the job done of creating a new magazine most effectively. I wrote Werner Erhard a letter requesting that he give us a scholarship—we were short on money at the time, and we certainly all couldn't afford to pay $250 to take the training. And they were considerate enough to give us that scholarship. I think their faith was based on the Erhard interview that we ran in the *East West Journal* in September 1974.

EWJ: So then you did the training. What was it like for you?
RH: I went into the training knowing everything that I learned in the training. I also went into the training having experienced very little of the things that I had learned before going into the training. The training made it possible for me to take all the things that I had known as intellectual concepts and bright ideas and have them become experiences for me so that they became real in my life. In the process of the training, I felt those ideas begin to sort of strip away. And at the same time that they became stripped away, they were sort of reborn and came alive. I'm talking specifically about taking responsibility for your life, for knowing that you are the cause of your own experience and that someone out there isn't doing it to you, and that what-

ever happens to you, you put out there in some form and in some form it's always coming back to you.

There was a moment in the training when my mind stopped, and there were moments when my mind resumed its motion. I had all kinds of realizations about how linear my thinking and perspective had been. It was in those moments, when my mind shut off, that I got it. Buddha said that there are three trillion thoughts that go through a person's mind in the blink of an eye, and if you can experience having no thoughts going through your mind for three seconds, you enter into samadhi. I don't think I experienced that for a full three seconds but I experienced that for a moment, and I'm sort of prone to saying that that moment existed outside of time. It didn't really exist within the framework of the class. In the moment when my mind shut off, I experienced full consciousness.

Following the training, that experience of full consciousness sort of catalyzed a semipermanent state of meditation in which I began to notice more things and to become more conscious in more and more areas of my life. When I say "conscious," I mean that I just began to notice my "act"—I began to notice the things I did, whether in my relationships or in my work or in the way I dealt with my body, and many other areas as well. I began to clean it up, which means that very rapidly I felt that my life began to take off and to expand, and the process of transformation really accelerated.

Then I decided to write a book about est. It was such a fascinating subject. The closer I looked at est, the closer I looked at myself and the more I'd have to apply consciousness to what was going on in my life. For example, while I was writing about broken agreements in the training, all the broken agreements in my life would start to be reactivated. And then I would set about cleaning those broken agreements up, whether by writing a letter to someone or paying a traffic ticket or completing a cycle of unfinished work.

The problems of acceleration were actually much greater

then than immediately after the training. It led me to consider that perhaps the results of the training were not automatic. Although they say that the purpose of the est training is to transform your ability to experience so that the things you've been putting up with clear up just in the process of life itself, it seemed that that would only happen to me inasmuch as I was willing to apply consciousness to specific areas of my life in a very disciplined way, and to take responsibility for what was going on, even if it seemed that someone up there was making it difficult for me—someone or something. From that, I began to conclude that est worked, and it didn't work—that taking responsibility for my life worked. Ultimately my relationship to est created a space or served the purpose for me to begin to notice that in the process of taking responsibility for my life, my life began to expand and my process of transformation to accelerate.

EWJ: But that's not necessarily the results of the training?
RH: I'm not saying that it's not the results of the training; I'm saying that the transformations that I've gone through since taking the training were primarily a result of my willingness to take responsibility for my life. The training created a space for me to become aware that that's what I had to do to make my life work. It created the awareness that that is what works. It didn't make it happen—I made it happen by taking responsibility for my life.

EWJ: Does est work for everyone?
RH: I have no idea whether the number of people it works for is five or fifty thousand. I've observed that most people who take the training do experience a transformation in their lives—to what extent I can't judge for anyone else. If I hadn't taken responsibility for using the things that I got out of est in a very disciplined way, I don't think that my transformation, at this point, would have been anywhere near as great as it has been.

EWJ: How about the est organization itself, and the way they operate?

RH: In my experience of dealing with the est organization, I sometimes found contradictions between how they operated and est's stated purpose of open and clear communication. There's a passage in R.D. Laing's *The Politics of Experience* that says that there are more and more people talking about communication, and communicating less and less. I found the est organization very effective when it came to telling me how to communicate, and when I employed the things I learned in the est training, they did—and do—facilitate my ability to communicate. As a journalist, however, I found the est organization very unwilling to communicate about itself. In some instances dealing with the est organization was like dealing with the secrecy of the CIA or the Pentagon.

EWJ: Does the comparison hold in terms of the use and abuse of power?

RH: I want to be clear here that est is making a very valuable contribution to the lives of many people, but I also want to be clear that there is a very authoritarian power structure being built up around est. I see Werner Erhard being given a great deal of power. I also see that Werner Erhard is human, and while I don't think he is abusing that power himself, I think that the organization is expanding so quickly that there is always the possibility that he will give power to someone who might not know how to use it with the highest degree of integrity.

EWJ: Do you feel that there's a backlash occurring with regard to est now? Many of the early articles that appeared on est were fairly favorable, but as time has gone by, I've seen a more critical response.

RH: Let's put it this way: What I find in reading the articles that have recently been written about est is that most of the writers don't know what to say about it. They don't know how to deal with it. So what they do, because they don't know how to look at it, is come out of their own point of view and come off by trying to judge it and evaluate it and make conclusions about it. If you can make conclusions about something and analyze it, you don't have to think about it anymore. You can just sort of tuck it away. Most of the things that are written about est have very little to do with est and have a lot to do with the individual writer's own attitude and tendency to make conclusions and judgments about things.

What I'm doing in my book is sharing my experience of the training, the seminar programs, and the est organization, recreating that experience as it happened. Proceeding without evaluations or judgments, I have come up with a lot of unanswered questions about est that the est organization was reluctant to answer. I will say, however, that I experienced Werner Erhard's love and support in writing my book. Its purpose is to make the greatest possible contribution to other people's lives.

EWJ: Est says that the training isn't necessary, that no one has to take it. Do you see other things going on today where individuals are experiencing change in their lives similar to that catalyzed by your est experience?

RH: I think there are many other ways that people can experience the same kinds of experiences that happen in est. Before I got involved with est, I was involved with many different aspects of the things that are associated with the new consciousness—a rainbow of different techniques and possibilities for experiencing experience and becoming increasingly conscious. Est was like a laser: it took all the light in the rainbow and condensed it into a single beam.

Chapter I

NOTHING LIKE YOU'VE EVER SEEN

At 7:45 P.M. I was winding around the upper levels of the concrete spiral, frantically looking for a place to park my Volvo. I was over fifteen minutes late. Werner Erhard, founder of est (Erhard Seminar Training) was giving a "Special Guest Seminar" across the street at the Sheraton-Boston. I had heard that latecomers received reproachful glances from the est staff and it was not my intention to suffer any embarrassment for such a seemingly innocent offense. Neither did I want to be late. I had waited many months to hear the man that a political and entertainment reporter from the *Denver Post* called "the most charismatic person I have ever seen."

I finally found a place to park on the roof of the garage. I ran down the stairs and across Dalton Street. It was a windy evening in the early part of March and the air was brisk. I pulled the collar of my denim jacket up around my neck and didn't stop running till I reached the reception area of the Grand Ballroom.

I was almost out of breath when I asked the graduate at the door (a young man whose jaws seemed locked in a permanent smile) if he would grant me the privileges of the press. I assumed his consent, but he stared emptily into my eyes. "Do you have anything to show that the world agrees you are a member of the working press?"

"I don't even carry a driver's license."

"Then you'll have to buy a ticket," he responded in a pre-programmed voice, indicating that I should move on.

"But I don't even carry a driver's license!"

"Then you'll have to buy a ticket."

There was something about his manner that irritated the hell out of me. He was cocksure, arrogant, and—after all, who was he? I stared back at him with my stomach dropping, but he had begun to ignore me.

But he didn't seem to notice.

Raising my voice, I said, with a sense of outrage, "You deserve a punch in the mouth."

"Thank you," he said. "Please see one of the people at the tables about your ticket."

He pointed to a bank of green folding tables strung around two-thirds of the room like a necklace. There must have been at least a hundred est graduates sitting behind them. They were helping guests fill out forms imprinted with the est logo—three bending orchid leaves, the Oriental symbol of love, refinement, and the perfect human being—and providing spaces for each guest's name, address, and telephone number. I heard one woman graduate tell the person in front of me, "Your mailbox will never be empty again."

Having spent a good part of my working life trying to keep the top of my desk free of mail that I never knew what to do with, I was more than a bit apprehensive. But I had had my fill of confrontations with the est staff for one night. And I filled out my card without a fuss. Still, when the very attractive graduate who was assisting me reached for a name tag, I was laid back.

"Everyone here is wearing a name tag. What we'd like you to do is to wear a name tag this evening," she replied.

The name tag made me uncomfortable but I put it on and stood at the entrance doors to the ballroom with about thirty other people waiting to be let in to the main event.

I had read in one article about est that Werner Erhard was "casually, but impeccably dressed." Casually, yes. He wore a white body shirt open wide at the neck, but from my vantage point in the wings of the Grand Ballroom, I couldn't see any other details. There were over two thousand people in the room and the excitement being generated by the thirty-nine-year-old Erhard, formerly known as Jack Rosenberg, who says that his guru is the physical universe, was almost hypnotizing.

Werner, as the graduates call him, was moving back and forth across the expansive stage with the grace of a house cat and the power of a mountain lion.

His voice seemed electrified by its own certainty, his delivery an echoing series of thunderbolts, his every sentence a complete and seductive thought.

Drawing upon an analogy from Alan Watts who said that human beings have a notion that they are tubes, and that the purpose of life is to put something in one end and take it out the other, Erhard let his puck fly with a scatological shot. The only reason most people have for waking up in the morning he said is because they either have to eat or go to the bathroom. While Erhard isn't prone to making claims for himself or est, the one claim he is often tempted to make is that when people take the training they find out that they are not a tube. In a similar sense, they also find out that they are not their problems.

"I am not my problems - - - - -," the thought seemed to soar through my mind like a rocket, cracking an emotional sound barrier with a psychic boom. There was a moment of clarity, of "space," but before I could figure it out, Erhard shifted gears into a nonstop verbal overdrive and I spun away with him.

We move through life totally resigned to the story or soap opera of our lives. It may be tolerable, but no matter how good life gets, and no matter how many symbols of being o.k. we acquire, it all lacks the experience of being complete. It is still a scenario; and though the characters may change as each episode builds upon the next, the story remains a never ending Search for Tomorrow.

And then sometimes we stumble, as if by accident, (Erhard backs up a few paces on stage) and catch a glimpse of things as they really are.

Erhard returns to his original position; he is going to do it right. He backs up again, only this time his legs slide out from under him, and the audience swoons like a circus crowd as he hits the floor with a thump. Applause. Laughter. Erhard is funny.

You trip as if by accident, and you are suddenly knocked off the position in the scenario which is keeping you stuck in your point of view.

The world stops as Don Juan says and you get off it; you stop seeing yourself as the victor, or even the victim of your problems; and you begin to get a sense of your own unbridled perfection.

It all starts with telling the truth, and the est training creates a space in which you not only feel safe in telling the truth, but one in which you are likely to have a direct experience of who you really are.

After about an hour of Erhard's catapulting monologue, the audience seems stoned into utter silence.

Erhard took his foot off the accelerator, reducing the centrifugal force that seemed to be blowing everybody's mind away on the curves. He opened himself to questions, and there were more than a few participants who had the courage to stand up in front of two thousand people and face Werner.

I was not one of them, although I wanted to be. I sat back in my seat trying to formulate the perfect question to defeat Erhard and win the respect of the audience. I had one or two possibilities which I had written down in my notebook earlier, but I was too nervous to memorize them, and only by memorizing them could I have gotten them out. Before long, I began to observe the game I was playing, and I moved on to something else. It wouldn't have worked anyway. Dealing with the ultimate questions people have about the training and about life is Erhard's business, and he handles them with the airconditioned ease of a veteran truck driver who must move his eighteen-wheeled rig through Boston's Haymarket Square on a Friday afternoon in the middle of August. The tighter the jam, the sooner Erhard seems to find the space to move out on the expressway. Erhard is cool.

He called on a lanky young man dressed in army surplus who looked as though he might have just returned from a march on Washington (ten years earlier). The protester was clamoring from the balcony, "Why does the training cost two hundred and fifty dollars?" (That's right, two hundred and fifty dollars).

I expected him to flinch, but Erhard relaxed into the question with the poise of a Tai Chi master, and the verbal simplicity of a poet; because it does.

I was surprised, but the young man sat down with aplomb.

Erhard called on an older woman, your typical Mayflower Society material, Daughter of the American Revolution.

"What do you do with all that money, young man?" she asked in a voice that had been nurtured in the vicinity of Hahvahd Yahd.

"We spent it with a touch of class that might have been taken by some as impudence." Although est is structured as a profit-making organization, training costs are high and the corporation has never shown a profit. Recently, however, est has donated the net proceeds of two trainings to organizations that have demonstrated their ability to "serve

(Note: There are usually 240 people in each monthly training. A recent est bulletin states that there are now over 12,000 people waiting to take the training in eleven est cities: San Francisco—Erhard's home base, Los Angeles, Honolulu, Aspen, Denver, San Diego, New York, San Jose, Washington, Berkeley, Oakland, Boston, and most recently, Chicago.)

people." Including six additional trainings that have been given at no cost to participants in underprivileged areas, this represents a contribution well over $300,000, or ten per cent of est's total revenues for 1974.

I was delighted with his answer. I had long grown weary of those countercultural doctrines intoning that all those who would do something for the good of society must give up everything and be penniless. Most of the people I know who have tried this approach have usually wound up on welfare, supported by the very institutions for which they have so much disdain.

There are over sixty-five thousand people, including myself, who have now taken est. I would say that almost everyone complains about the price of the training before taking it, and almost no one does afterward.

Eight weeks after I left the Sheraton-Boston that night, I found out why there are few complaints. The training works. The value my wife and I got out of it would have made it a knockdown bargain at twice the price.

What did we get out of it? A much better relationship with each other. It was only a short time ago that my wife told me she was "totally happy" in our marriage, "completely satisfied" in our relationship. I couldn't believe it, a month earlier she was ready to leave me. Curiously enough, when I filled out a form at the April pre-training about what I expected to get out of est, I randomly wrote down "a better relationship with my wife"; the phrase "cosmic consciousness" seemed too verbose. And yet I hardly thought about her or our marriage during the entire two weekends in which the training took place. I wrote down "a better relationship," and that's what I "got."

Similar things happen to almost everyone who takes the training. For some people, the results are immediate; for others, it takes a little longer. According to Erhard's observations, almost everyone who takes the training begins to experience significant transformations in his life in less than a year. But Don Cox, president of est, former general manager of the Coca-Cola Bottling Company of California and a former faculty member of the Harvard Business School, is quick to point out, "No claims, guarantees, or promises are made for the est training. That would be inconsistent with the purpose of the training."

What is the purpose of the training? "The purpose of the est training is to transform your ability to experience living, so that the situations you have been trying to change or have been putting up with clear up just in the process of life itself." Further, according to est trainer Brendan Hart, once you take the training there doesn't have to be a lot of effort involved: "It is when you get out of effort and struggle that things do begin to clear up!"

One graduate I spoke to said, "In the training, you get to take a look at that part of yourself that isn't working." Although to look is not always to see, Erhard says that if you look at anything long enough and tell the truth about it, it will disappear.

Looking at that part of oneself that isn't working is like peeling the layers of skin off an onion.

At the moment that you "get" the training, you know what the *self* really is.

When Erhard was interviewed by the *Boston Globe* he was asked, "To whom do you owe your allegiance, yourself or society?" He replied:

> I would answer that question by saying that your responsibility is to yourself. But then you have to define "self" in one of two ways. You can take a limited view of yourself or a cosmic view of yourself. In a cosmic view of yourself, the self begins to extend out to include other systems; it begins to extend out to include the world.

What most people seem to get out of est is a larger view of themselves, one that is based on an experience of their own centers, without any of the "racket" that is created by that "wild monkey"—as Buddhists call it—the mind.

When I woke up the morning after the training and said to myself, "I feel great today!" I didn't hear a little voice inside my head saying, "It can't last." But it doesn't. There is only one guarantee that I have ever heard a trainer make. If you go up after the training, you will eventually come down, and vice versa. When the mountain is high, the valley is low. The training has nothing to do with being high or low. It has to do with being wherever you are.

Do the results of the training last? Don Cox is ready to admit that "there is a natural tendency to be skeptical of graduates of a four-day training who indicate that they have experienced a transformation whereby their lives begin to be more fulfilling and to work better; also that the improvement actually increases over time.

"And yet," says Cox, "that is what graduates report time after time."

Studies of est graduates have been conducted by respected independent researchers, including a survey of fourteen hundred est graduates that was headed by Dr. Robert Ornstein, a noted psychological researcher and faculty member of the Langley Porter Neuropsychiatric Institute of California. The results of these studies, according to Ornstein, are consistent with est's own statements.

Judging from my personal experience, I would have to agree that the beneficial results of the training do actually increase over time. It has been over a year now since I took the training, and I am well past the fascination stage. A year may not seem like enough time to draw conclusive evidence as to how long the results of the training last, but in the words of one staff member who was quoted in the *Denver Post*, "All we can answer is that it works for at least three and a half years because that's how long we've been giving the training."

What is the training about? Trainer Randy McNamara says, "It's about nothing," but it's "nothing" like you ain't ever seen.

Chapter II
MIRACLES AND REALIZATIONS

Christ! How many movements before had run into the selfsame problem. Every vision, every insight . . . came out of the new experience . . . and the kairos . . . and how to tell it! How to get it across to the multitudes who have never had this experience themselves? *You couldn't put it into words.* You had to create the conditions in which they would feel an approximation of *that feeling*, the sublime *kairos*. You had to put them into ecstasy . . . Buddhist monks immersing themselves in cosmic love . . . Hindus zonked out on Bhakti . . . ecstatics flooding themselves with Krishna . . . Christians off in Edge City through Ghostic onanism or the heart of Jesus or the Child Jesus with the running sore—or—
—TOM WOLFE,
The Electric Kool-Aid Acid Test

Or—or—est graduates at a post-training. The atmosphere is one to rival—and go a universe beyond—the ecstatic aftermath of the old "acid tests" of Ken Kesey, and the Merry Pranksters. Gathered together in the Constitution Lounge of the Commodore Hotel in New York City are 250 people. They are not graduates of a chemical feast (burnt out by an experience of the One, the All, in a totally wound-up, mind-blown state of enlightenment), but of the August C est training, now in its final stretch.

Demographically, they range from long-haired college dropouts of the Lower East Side, to middle-aged housewives from East Islip and Southampton, to stylish Manhattan secretaries, to self-made business executives (advertising, publishing, hardware, software) from White Plains and other hamlets of Westchester County.

Although they are as typical as any group of American middle-class whites, there is no generation gap here, only people who in their sharing have served as surrogate mothers and fathers, daughters, sisters and brothers, sons and lovers. More than half the people in the room have shit-eating grins on their faces. And behind that grin is the bright aura of anticipation. "How do I know I got it?" They are all here to find out. "What happened in the training?" They are also here to "create the conditions" so that the hundred or so guests that are in the room can experience "an approximation of *that feeling, the sublime kairos*" of aliveness, completion, and satisfaction that they "got" in the est training.

And then out of nowhere, just as he appeared on the first day of the training, comes Hal, right down the center aisle, Hal who had been their trainer during the second weekend, Hal who had "given it to them" like nobody's business; here's Hal dressed in white woolen pants and a tailored English sports jacket that is almost a half a size too small. Hal Isen reaches the stage.

"Hello!" Hal bellows in a bass-baritone. (All the trainers speak in a bass-baritone, straining a little so it sounds as if they've got broken glass in their throats.)

"Hellooooo!!!" the audience bellows back 250 decibels louder. And then—wait a minute, what are we doing?—graduates in every corner of the room rise as if someone were playing "Hail to the Chief" and give Hal a standing ovation—a touching and spontaneous gesture of their appreciation. Hal cracks open a big smile, not the sly, crushing, "you bunch of assholes," trainer smile that he had given them a week before, but a smile that seems to convey a sense of "We're all one now." Hal leans back and applauds the audience, nodding with a sense of pride.

And then the booming bass-baritone from Northwest Washington, D. C.:

"I'd like to welcome you here tonight, those of you who are graduates, and those of you who are guests. If you are a guest, I'd like you to know that the graduates and I spent some time together"—the smile again—"so we know each other." (Applause/laughter.) "The purpose of tonight's meeting, if you are a guest, is to answer all your questions about est, and if you are a graduate, to find out what's so about you now. You spent sixty hours in the training and some of you probably aren't sure what happened. So we're going to talk about that and what the exact results of the training are." (Unexplained laughter from the graduates.) "We'll also handle what's so about the future, and what you can do to accelerate the movement that you experienced in the training.

"What I'd like to do now is to open a space for those of you to share what's been going on since I saw you last." (Hands are raised in almost every row.) "Yeah, William."

William gets up out of the first row left. He takes a microphone that is given to him by someone from the est "logistics team," and makes a sweeping turn toward the audience. "Wow! I've just got to thank Hal again for what happened here Sunday night." (Sunday was the last night of the training.) "I have been so—high!" As he says this, his voice moves up a pitch.

"I went back to work on Monday, and found out that not only did I have the big promotion that I have been hoping to get, but the boss calls me into his office and tells me starting tomorrow I'm gonna start doing his job too. It just blew me away."

clapclapclapclapclapclapclapclapclapclap
clapclapclapclapclapclap
clapclapclap

(It's a tradition in est that you either clap or throw money after people "share.")

William continues: "And then last night I crashed. I didn't know that being alive and being happy could exhaust me so much. Wow! It's really been great."

clapclapclapclapclapclapclapclap
clapclap

William sits down. The atmosphere in the room is "manic," although in est such words are taboo.

Hal looks around the room and calls, "Yeah, Janet. Stand up and take the microphone." (A logistics person races down the aisle, hands Janet the microphone, and drops out of sight.)

"Ever since taking the training, I've been experiencing tremendous love for my fellow man. And I asked someone I knew, 'Do you love me?' And his face vanished and Hal's face popped up. And I've only known Hal for two days, and I feel he loves me. And I love him."

clapclapclapclapclapclapclapclapclapclapclap
clapclapclap
clapclap

"Beautiful, Janet, very nice," Hal says, trying not to take things too personally. "Clarence? . . ."

"I'd like to say that I got tremendous value out of the training. Yesterday, I woke up feeling really empty"—in the Zen sense of the word, this means the silent zero in search of a sound—"and I said to myself, 'Nothing's really changed.'" (Laughter.) "And it's all totally different."

clapclapclapclapclapclapclapclap
clapclap

Hal smiles knowingly, "Linda."

"I've been having migraine headaches and carrying around a pain in my back for the last ten years. And they're gone. They're just gone! I don't know where they went, or if they'll ever be back, but I do know that they're gone. Incredible!"

"Fabulous, Linda, fabulous," says Hal.

clapclapclapclap
clapclap
clap

"Candice..."

"I said good-bye to my psychiatrist today. And he said, 'Are you certain that you want to leave?' And I said yes, and he said, 'Why?' And I said, 'Because I'm certain.' He said, 'How do you know? What part of you is certain?' 'Because I'm certain.' He said, 'I'm frightened that you want to leave.' And I said, 'Good. Experience it.'" (Appalling laughter.)

clapclapclapclapclapclapclap
clapclap
clapclapclapclap

Hal calls on Sherman.

"Well, Sunday night, when we graduated, I was down, and after we graduated, I went home and I was still down. I was all hung up about something that came up for me during the first weekend. I just couldn't get the two weekends together.

"The next morning I got up. Took a shower. I was shaving, standing there looking in the mirror. And it was like a thunderbolt hit me. I started laughing. I was hysterical. I couldn't believe it. I stood there looking in the mirror and said, 'I got it! I—got it.' And I realized that in my whole life I've never before seen people for what they were. I've always tried to change them. And I saw that you can't change anyone. All you can do is accept them for what they are."

"Great, Sher—"

        clapclapclapclapclapclap
              clapclap
                   clap
                        clapclap

Hal points to Penny, extending his forearm toward her like a traffic cop. Penny is in her late forties, with a background in theater—a trained voice from the word *go-oh*.

"I don't know anything about mystical experiences. I've never had any before. And I've been having mystical experiences for the last week. I mean, I have been through the universe and *ba-ack*. And I ask myself if these things are significant? And I know the answer is *no-oh*. They're no more significant than chocolate pudding."

clapclapclapclapclapclapclapclapclapclapclapclapclap
      clapclapclapclapclapclapclap
            clapclapclapclap

"Stay with it, Penny," Hal says. "Madeline . . . what would you like to share?"

"Unlike the rest of you, I haven't been happy. I haven't been positive, and it's all not falling into place. I've been very"—wiping her eyes with a handkerchief—"depressed, very, very depressed. There's been so much pain and sadness—"

"Thank you, Madeline. Very nice. . . ."

                    clapclapclapclap
                clapclapclapclapclapclap
                              clapclap

"Joanie." Hal calls on a woman in the back of the room.
"I got out of the training feeling like the first thing I wanted to do was call my ex-husband. So I called him up and said, 'Barry, I love you.' And he said, 'Whah? Are you drunk?' And I said, 'No. And you're with Denise. And that's OK.' "
The audience belly-laughs.

                    clapclapclapclapclap
                        clapclapclapclap
                            clap

"Sal."
"I've been crashing and cresting, crashing and cresting; and mostly I've noticed how I've been able to be here now—totally concentrated in the movement—no sense of time. It's a completely different framework than I have ever existed in before. The training really works."

                clapclapclapclapclapclapclap
                        clapclapclap
                            clap

"Great," Hal says. "I'd like to ask one more person to share before the guests leave the room with their seminar leaders. OK, Steve, how about you?" Steve looks like a white Fats Waller, Mr. Five-by-Five in the flesh.
"Several times during the last couple of days I've asked myself if I'd 'gotten' it. The answer was always no. And then I'd be walking along the street and I'd look into a store window and see my own reflection." (It had to be by accident—for obvious reasons.) "And I'd say"—he cracks up—"this guy didn't get it!"

The room overboiled with laughter.

"The other day I read an article about est, at the end of which the author wrote, 'And I love Werner Erhard.' I thought this was completely crazy. Gonzo! But you know something. I love Werner Erhard too." (more laughter.)

clapclapclapclapclapclapclapclapclapclapclap
                    clapclapclapclapclapclap
                              clapclapclapclap . . .

After the guests had left the room, Hal looks at the audience with a devilish grin and says, "OK. Now let's talk about the Good Shit."

As I left Hal's post training that night, I experienced the same sense of exhilaration that I had felt several months earlier after seeing Erhard for the first time at the Sheraton Boston.

The Beginning is the End
(March 1975)

Back in the red-walled cavern of the Grand Ballroom, he ended the evening with an expression of gratitude that cut through his prevailing image as a used car dealer, in prepackaged, freeze-dried enlightenment. It was as if someone had pressed the dissolve change on a slide projector. Superimposed above this guru in Brooks Brothers clothing, I was beginning to perceive a picture of a completely different man.

He began by saying that he didn't come to the event to sell us on taking the training; adding that life would work out for us if we didn't take the training. Not only would life work out for him if we didn't take the training, he said life would work out for us if we didn't take the training.

clapclapclap
clapclapclapclap
clap

He thanked us for being there, for our time and our attention; he considered it a gift. But what he really wanted to thank us for, and not as the source or spokesman of est, was the space that we created by being willing to be with him.

Applause.

Beautiful. He said that he wanted us to know that in the space that we gave him, he was able to create satisfaction and completion for himself.

clapclapclapclapclap
clapclapclap
clap

I couldn't comprehend my experience of Erhard's gratitude. I had been thanked by politicians. I had been thanked by entertainers, by silver-tongued swamis, and silent saddhus. I had been thanked by the guy in the gas station that night, and by the attendant at the toll booth, and by the woman in the parking lot for whom I had held open the elevator door. I had been thanked by hundreds of other people I've done favors for. And this was the first time in my life that I was able to experience another person's gratitude totally—a person who had never known me, or talked to me, nor even seen my face, in an audience of over two thousand people. What's more, almost every other person that I shared this with that evening had a similar experience. Believers, disbelievers, and even those who did not know whether to believe or not—almost all seemed to take his words as if they meant something to each of them personally. They did. And for many it would be the beginning of a long-standing relationship, one that would go way beyond the traditional concepts of guru/disciple, dealer in what one journalist has called "psychological snake oil."

Enrollments that night were only ten percent, but as the evening ended there were est staff members descending upon me from all directions. They were following me around like a pack of dogs; I was beginning to know what it's like to be a bitch in heat.

A tall, blond, lanky young man named Eric, head as big as a basketball, innocuous features, like vulcanized seams, the type who holstered a slide rule from his belt in high school, blocked my path to the door.

"Do you want to take the training?"

I had been impressed by Erhard, to say the least, and I was coming from a place where I could feel my identity being transferred to his. It was just like walking out of the theater after a knuckle-busting, pistol-popping, John Wayne movie. I was a "heeeero." And this guy, this dink in a green suit and white socks, was going to get the point.

"Do you want to take the training?" he asked again, as another feature-length fantasy began to flash through my mind.

"I'll take the training when I take the training," I answered, with all the sagebrush sagacity I could muster in a single tautological sentence.

I looked into his eyes—electric-blue, glassy eyes with whites the color of paraffin—to see if this veritably Zen statement of mine would make him blink. There was no movement at all of his eyes, not even a tiny quiver in the lids, and still there was something, a still-life impression of the being who looked through those eyes. They almost seemed to say, "Nobody home, nobody here at all." And then ... blink!

"Do you think you would get value out of this training?"

"I do. And I also think I would get value out of jumping in the Charles River, as long as there was someone there to fish me out."

"In the training there is no one there to fish you out." I thought, What the hell did he mean by that? Then he said, "Do you want to take the training?" All over again.

"Yeah, I wanna take the training, but I don't feel the slightest motivation to do so now. I'll take the training when I take the training." In case he had missed the sagacity of my point, I added, "I mean you do what you do when you do it."

He started to say something, a few words burbled from his lips, and then his mind seemed to stop. Without wasting any of his intention on words, he threw the full force of his being into his eyes. No one had ever stared at me like this before, not even the people at Arica. It was like looking into the surface of a highly polished mirror. Somehow, through the surface of his eyes, eyes that seemed connected to the center of the universe, I was seeing the most hidden, God-awful parts of myself. It made my flesh crawl.

I wanted to move away, but that would have been an admission of my gut reaction. I tried to quiet my mind, but it kept on playing that tape, the same old silent soliloquy, "Nobody home, there is nobody home. There is nothing going on with me. What's going on with you??????????????" I couldn't even guess.

Who was this guy? And how could he be doing this to me?

"Do you think you'd get value out of this training if you took it now?" he asked after a while.

"Yes, I'm sure I would—but I don't feel the slightest inclination to take it now." I thought I was being true to my own being; after all, my own credibility with myself was in question.

Still relatively cool on the surface, I screwed up my eyes, literally screwed them up. Everything went out of focus as I returned the stare. If he was doing it to me, I was going to do it back. But no matter how hard I tried, I couldn't focus on anything higher than his neck. And the more I looked at his neck, the more I could feel my own center rising up into my throat.

I flashed on a picture of myself with a big inner tube around my head. His presence seemed to suck at my insides

—at a lifetime of pressing the repress button, splitting, projection, fear-anger-guilt-anxiety—like a supercharged industrial vacuum cleaner (whoosh!!!) in a single emotional blast.

The floor seemed to disappear beneath my feet. At least I couldn't feel anything below my knees; and still on the surface I was a fantasied combination of John Wayne, Colt .45, and Toshiro Mifune slashing with a samurai sword, so the lovely young lady who had accompanied me for the evening wouldn't see what was really going on. And so I could pretend that what was really going on wasn't really going on.

It must have been a good act, because by this time a group of people had gathered around to watch the scene.

Always willing to cater to an audience, I raised my voice and let into my adversary. He was caught off guard. "Look, Eric, you either take this training or you don't take this training. There are no reasons to take this training, and there are no good reasons not to take it. Erhard said that nobody needs this training. I certainly don't need it. If I did, I would take it. And if I ever do, I'll let you know."

Presto! Eric seemed to crack open. His basketball head seemed deflated. He tried to throw me another hook shot with his eyes, but the ball just wouldn't bounce. He was in vital shock. Paralysis. Going solid. The seams on his face seemed to fold up around the corners of his mouth, and at that point I knew that it was all over.

He said, "Thank you" (why the hell was he thanking me?) and walked away.

Externally, I was the victor, but inside I felt a measure of shame. Smartass! I had put Eric down to escape his confrontation and to make myself look good. I had been putting people down for my whole life to make myself look good. I had masked it in the role of the father and in the role of the boss, the power of position, position of guru, "true friend"—anything to make the other be wrong and me right. Except that it didn't work. It never worked because inside I was afraid, a barking dog and a bowl of Jello.

When it was all over with Eric, I looked toward the bystanders for approval, for smiling accolades. But before I could utter a word, there was another est staff member staring me right in the face, and I was into it all over again. Except that I can't remember a thing that was said, because I was almost totally unconscious of whom I was talking to. I was still back there with Eric, slinking away. I wanted to go and find him and apologize, but I let it slide.

The crowd hung on while my second antagonist drifted away. I was no more aware of his disappearance than I had been of his presence. Then a casual friend of mine with crow's feet in the corners of his eyes appeared out of nowhere. "How ya doin', Keith?" I said. Keith had a Mr. Natural appearance, not the kind that is defined by Big Smith, OshKosh, or Levi overalls, but by a certain inner glow. It came from within—alpha, beta, Bucks County, Pennsylvania.

I had heard that Keith was a diehard est graduate. But I was so glad to see a friendly face after my last two encounters that it didn't seem to get in the way.

And then he asked me, "Are you going to take the training?" in an offhanded, conversational way that took me off the defensive.

I told him that I might take the training in the future. "It might make a good story. . . ."

What happened next—well, it wasn't what Keith said, it was who he is, and where he was coming from. I experienced the tone of his being in much the same way that I had experienced Erhard's gratitude, and it was in that collection of moments that I decided to take the training.

I told Keith that the only thing that was standing in the way of me and the training was the admission price. "I've got a wife and three kids and I can't afford—"

"I got that," he said. "I'll put up the thirty dollars deposit. Sign up for the April training, and if you don't have the money by then, you can always take it some other time."

I was so taken by Keith's offer that I accepted it and signed up for the April training that night.

We talked about this meeting six months later in a nonstop four-hour conversation that took place on Interstate 95, heading south toward New York for another est event. Keith had overheard me talking to the two other est graduates that evening in the Sheraton-Boston. He was one of the bystanders to whom I unknowingly looked for approval.

Keith took a swig from a bottle of Heinke apple juice and said, "I saw you building up to a powerful state of indifference. And just before I walked over to you, I gave up completely on the idea that you would ever be persuaded to take the training. There was nothing to do but give up."

I wouldn't have been "persuaded" to take the training. I was too caught up in my game of one-upsmanship at that time to really listen to what people had to say. By being willing to be with me, Keith allowed me to be.

I don't know who said that "giving up is all there is to give," but in this case, it created a space for me to be in the training.

Chapter III

WHEN YOU KNOW
THAT YOU DON'T KNOW

Gautama Buddha got it under the bodhi tree. And Jesus of Nazareth got it in the wilderness. The prophet Mohammed got it wrapped in his blanket on Mount Hara, and Moses when he saw the burning bush at Horeb. Francis Bacon got it at his desk, and Balzac during a visit to Madame Surville. Walt Whitman got it in the leaves of grass and J. P. Morgan on Wall Street. Don Juan got it in the mountains of Mexico, and Werner Erhard while driving across the Golden Gate Bridge. Thank you, Father, for what we are about to receive.

On the morning of April 26, 1975, 250 people were lined up outside Conference Room A to "get it" at the Howard Johnson's Motor Lodge, 200 Stuart Street, Boston. Lined up like summer tourists at a fried-clam stand, like baseball fans outside the city's Fenway Park, like stargazers crowding around Grauman's Chinese Theater, they were here to take the training, to be enlightened, or in the vernacular, "lightened up." Erhard makes no attempt to hide the fact that he is in the business of selling enlightenment. But there was no consciousness of that here. The people were here for reasons that were as unknown to them as to anybody else, here to take the training, to try anything that might make their lives work, even if it cost them two weekends and a couple of hundred bucks.

"Sure, I know your life works," Rod Logan would say during the second weekend. "Then why are your relationships so lousy?" Whatever the reasons were, they were ostensible. They were here because they thought they needed this training or because they thought they didn't need this training and they wanted to make sure.

Howard Johnson's, your Friendly Host of the Highways; Howard Johnson's, also listed as 57 Park Plaza—a visible apparition of all that Lewis Mumford, Murray Bookchin, and William Irwin Thompson have said is wrong with the twentieth century: concrete, steel, and glass; a totally rational, uniform environment in the midst of cultural insanities. The building is diagonally across the street from the Greyhound bus station and Boston's "Combat Zone," where pimps, pushers, and the police play hide and seek until the transparent light of dawn forces the action back into the cellars of Washington Street. It is the very same street on which the fathers of the American Revolution were inspired to hang their lantern from the Old North Church—"one if by land, two if by sea"—to fight for the rights of self-determination as well as for "life, liberty, and the pursuit of happiness." It was a valiant *effort*, and as *effort* it had all come down to this: a nation of people who were stuck out there in the illusion that the only route to satisfaction was more—more is better, better is more. The faces of the people who greeted the early morning shoppers in Kresge's, Jordan's, and Filene's basement were gray; no matter how much makeup they were wearing, still gray; no matter how much blue pencil they had rubbed on their eyelids before boarding the city's subway system, still gray, aura of gray. The Japanese call it the color of death. It was the price they had to pay for more. Aliveness, satisfaction? It had been squeezed right down the tubes of mascara and Super-Luscious Liquid Blush. More—more—more is better, better is more.

If the people who stood outside Conference Room A that morning hadn't decided to take the training this weekend, they might have been standing outside Gilchrist's or Kennedy's on Washington Street instead. There were few who understood the implications of what they were about to receive, or gave a thought to the place in which they were about to receive it. "No," the trainers would say later, "it ain't in the form"; but neither was it any accident that Werner Erhard decided to package his four-day "total-immersion experience" in rooms like Conference Room A, the same room that had served the Sunshine Biscuit Company, the New England Bridge Club, the Wiseburg-Rochelle dinner, the Phillips-McClarity wedding, the American Optical Company, the B'nai Brith Cinema Lodge, and the Glass Workers Union Local 1044, in the previous month.

How many saints and saddhus had attained enlightenment on a snowcapped mountain or a river bank or in a coconut grove and had become so attached to the "spirit of place" that they forgot that the experience was within them? How many unknown milarepas, marpas, bodhidhermas had spent more than twenty years making mudras, never to come out of their caves? How many had wandered the face of the earth from Jerusalem to Mecca, to Rancho de Taos and Esalene, to spacey Big Sur, only to discover that when they returned to that special place and sat under the ginkgo trees, it was never the same. They had "lost it." The experience had evaporated into the past, and they would never, until hell froze over, be able to "get it" again.

Were all the people standing outside Conference Room A waiting to be elevated into the mystical state of illumination? Some were; most were happy enough to have been elevated to the sixth floor where the conference rooms are located. They were here to take the training in a place that suggested a reasonable amount of security and comfort.

Howard Johnson had started his great chain of orange rooftops in New England, so they were familiar and at home with it, at least—the same way they felt familiar and at home whenever they heard the voice of their local TV newsman, Tom Ellis. "Good evening. This is Eye-Witness News." It was like being in their own living room, a "safe" and reasonable "space," except for the fact that they were still waiting in line while a team of est graduates checked over their registration forms and gave them name tags.

"Watches and timepieces. Watches and timepieces. Leave your watches and timepieces here," ordered a tall Tartar named Ivan, a high-powered executive at Raytheon Electronics. "Do you have a watch or a timepiece?" It seemed like an unreasonable request, and there are a lot of things about the training that are unreasonable, beginning with the amount of time that one has to spend in the training, that "safe" womb-like "space" that re-creates three and a half billion years of man's embryological development on this planet.

Were the trainees aware, once inside the conference room, how threatening that space would become? Had they any notion that in est "a safe space" meant a place to go through hell in a wheelbarrow that nobody would help you push until you were willing to recreate the place as heaven? I'm not sure, but one way or another, it was going to be a very powerful experience for all of them. And whether they knew it or not, most would be able to walk out of that same room the following weekend and be able to say, "I am the cause of my own experience," and mean it. They would not just be mouthing somebody else's words but their own experience of the way it really is. They had come into the training saying, "Somebody's out there doing it to me." This was the one attitude toward life that all the people now sitting in Conference Room A had in common. They had spent their whole lives playing the victim, but somehow in the process of the training, that attitude and the darkness that was in their faces would disappear. They would leave the training with their voltage all tuned up, lightened, radiant, no longer afraid to look other people in the eye. Their lives would not continue to be run by the fact that they had something they were ashamed of or didn't want other people to find out about. They would no longer have anything to hide. It would no longer make any difference.

Who ever thought you could "get" all this at Howard Johnson's, or the Ramada Inn, or the Statler Hilton, or the Sheraton-Boston, or any of the other hotels around the country where the trainings take place? Didn't you have to go to the mountains? Didn't you have to eat bark? And how many saints and saddhus had done just that only to find out that bark doesn't taste good, and that it's cold in winter and warm in summer. Rod Logan would say the following weekend, "Rocks are hard and water's wet." Oh, revelation of revelations! Most of the people would leave the room the following weekend with sore bottoms.

This is one of the ways in which the training produces its results. Though most of the people who take the training have previously gone through life looking for a place to sit down, he who is tired of sitting on his ass forever gets up and gets his life together. The form, processes, and results of the training are about as mystical as that—as revelatory as a sore bottom and the desire to get up, get up from one's chair, from one's tiresome position in a universe of infinite possibilities.

Still, for those people who don't particularly enjoy sitting in a hotel function room for sixty hours, and for those who have romantic, transcendental sensibilities, Erhard might have offered a few alternatives. He could have offered the former a training given on water beds, and the latter, one given on top of Mount Sinai or by the Wailing Wall in Jerusalem. But for most of the people now being told to "fill up the front row seating first"—local residents of the Boston area—the cost in either case would have been prohibitive. A round-trip ticket to Jerusalem on El Al Airlines goes for $599; add to that the price of a Hertz Rent-a-Camel, a tent with hot and cold running water, passport, meals, tips—and presto, the price of the training has been jacked up to $2,500. And you can still buy the $250 "getaway" weekend at Boston's 57 Park Plaza.

What a fantastic deal!

Although Conference Room A is the largest of the three conference rooms available at HoJo's (for under $300 a day), it measures a diminutive fifty-seven by sixty feet. The floors are covered with red carpet, and except in those areas where you can still see the scars of burning cigarettes crushed under the feet of conventioneers, the effect is not unpleasant. The red carpet and drapes warm the room, counterpointing the somewhat chilling effect of the white reinforced structural concrete beams that hang like a massive tic-tac-toe board from the ceiling. This room would be these people's entire universe for the next fifteen hours—a room without natural light, extraneous sound, or interruptions of any kind, a totally "safe space" in which to experience all that was going on with them that they had never allowed themselves to experience before. All the fear and all the anger, all the tears and all the joy, all the love and all the hatred, all the wars and all the peace—they would experience it all as the living truth, and in their own way know that the truth is all of it. They would experience it in such a way that it would all fit together—not as a concept, but as an experience. It would all become One.

The trainees took their appropriate seats.

The trainer himself would later acknowledge, "Everyone is sitting in exactly the seat I picked out for him. *Isn't that interesting?*" (A corollary of one of Werner Erhard's basic principles: that everything is perfect the way it is, and that wherever you are is the perfect place for you to be.)

A balding young man, wearing a permanently worried expression on his face and neatly pressed khaki pants, strolled up the center aisle. Upon reaching the front of the room, he introduced himself: "My name is David Norris and I'll be your training supervisor for this training." Then, like a marine boot-camp sergeant who had spent the last twenty-five years stationed on Parris Island, he proceeded to read off a list of "agreements" that we were supposed to make "our own." We were not to talk, take notes, smoke, chew gum, read, or sit beside anyone we knew very well before the start of the training. The agreements were later summarized by the trainer. "Keep your ass in the room, your sole"—pointing to the bottom of his shoes—"in the room, follow the instructions, and take what you get." These agreements were to be kept until the end of the training, except for one: that we would not discuss the form, content, or processes of the training with anyone but est graduates "until the end of it." ("That means when they bury you six feet under in a pine box.")

David concluded the list by saying, "We have observed that the agreements work, and they are one of the reasons why we can produce the results that we do in such a short period of time." Regarding confidentiality, we would be free to share our "experience" of the training, a word that was at that point still undefined, but later defined as "everything." ("That means all of it.")

Although it has been said in more than one article about est that this agreement is patently illegal, few graduates ever break it. It is one of the reasons that the training—and particularly the crucial last day—has rarely been reported in the press. The confidentiality question became an immediate source of confusion for me; or rather, it acted as a magnetic pole around which I began to experience all the confusion that was in my life prior to taking the training. Was I going to keep it or not? What if Woodward and Bernstein had had to make an agreement with Richard Nixon not to disclose any information about the Watergate breakin? We would still have a government run by desperate, unethical men. And hadn't Erhard recently replied to an article that referred to est as a "crypto-fascist, neo-Nazi organization" by saying that "a free press was a small price to pay for full communication" in a democratic society. And then there was Tom Wolfe, who wrote in *The New Journalism* that many reporters are so stricken by a sense of responsibility and obligation to their subjects that they eventually wind up embarrassing the very people they are trying to protect.

A writer needs enough ego to believe that what he is doing is as important as what anyone he might be writing about is doing. If he doesn't believe that his own writing is one of the most important activities going on in contemporary civilization, then he ought to move on to something else he thinks is . . . a welfare eligibility worker, or a clean-investment counselor for the Unitarian Church, or an abatement surveyor.

I wasn't ready to visit the Massachusetts Division of Employment Security for occupational counseling, and neither was I ready to make an agreement that I wasn't sure I was going to be able to keep. Though David had said that anyone who was not ethically in a position to keep the agreements should leave at the first break, I decided to hang in there anyway, at least until I could fully understand what the agreements were.

And then, not long after the first break, I began to realize that the form of the training is an illusion. It is like a photograph of an ice-cream cone. If you try to describe its flavor in terms of the form, data, or processes by which it is made, it is not likely that you will be understood. The only way to experience the satisfaction of eating an ice cream cone is to eat one. Similarly, the only way to experience the satisfaction that most people get out of taking the training is to take the training. As Erhard says, "That's what's so." It's also so that when you share something from your own experience that is particularly real for you, and it touches upon something that is particularly real in the experience of another, there is always the possibility of an "Aha! So that's what it's like!" I would like to be clear from the outset that this is what the training is *like*; it is not the training. I have made an agreement with myself not to discuss the form, content, or processes of the training, except from my own *experience*, and "That means all of it." I will discuss everything, with the exception of the specific processes themselves, not including the training itself as one of them.

Besides the fact that the training takes place in a hotel room and not atop Mount Fuji, there are several other significant aspects to its form.

First, during the training you have to spend more than sixty Spartan hours sitting in a hard-backed, unmerciful chair that doesn't care an iota whether you keep your agreements with it or not. Agreements with a chair? I should point out that it is the custom of many people who come into the training to slouch, slump, and squirm in their seats; and it doesn't take more than half a day in the training to permanently break them of the habit.

By that I mean that you can get away with slouching at a lecture, a movie theater, or at a ball game, anyplace where you are not required to be in your seat longer than your interest will keep you there; but if you have to sit in the same place approximately fifteen hours on any given day, it doesn't take you long to realize that if you don't sit with your spine straight, you are going to have one hell of an aching back in addition to a sore bottom.

Holy men and women have been sitting with their spines straight and "getting it" for the last five thousand years and then some. According to Chogyam Trungpa Rinpoche, a Buddhist meditation teacher, "When you sit with your spine straight, the energy (chi, prana, or life force) flows to you and through you more directly." Whether this is mystical whitewash for a still unexplained phenomenon, I am not in a position to say, but I am sure that it works, and more than half a million people who practice Transcendental Meditation would agree. To explain it simply: If you wanted to water your garden, would you use a hose that was twisted, bent, and wrapped around the wheel of your car, or would you use one that was supple and straight, a direct link to your tomato patch? Sitting with your spine straight gets the water out to the garden; classically, it's a way to get clear.

I should mention here that with the exception of certain processes that comprise a very small portion of the training, no one on the est staff ever asks anyone to sit up straight. Nor does everyone do it, and the results of the training would still be produced whether anyone did it or not.

So there has to be something else that makes the training work, and maybe it is the fact that, secondly, the trainees are given a maximum of one meal break a day, which usually takes place after eight or nine o'clock in the evening and sometimes not at all.

Jesus, Buddha, Mohammed, Moses, Isaiah, Mahatma Ghandi, and a long line of lesser notables all "got it" after a period of fasting, whereas some people have fasted and never gotten it at all—Wordsworth, Pushkin, Pascal, and Pliny, to name only a few. Although Erhard does not suggest fasting outside the training room, he points out that people will do anything to go unconscious, and one of the ways they will do that is by eating.

Assuming Erhard is correct in his observation, anyone who puts himself in the position of having to sit in a room with his spine straight for more than fifteen hours with absolutely nothing to eat, nothing to do, and nothing to do it with except his mind, is going to have to deal with some things in his life that make him very uncomfortable. The trainees go into the training with all their neurotic speed, with all their aggressions, and they are literally told to do nothing. And wouldn't it be nice if you could sneak out of the room and eat Westphalian ham, knockwurst, ice cream, peanut-butter crackers, or whatever it is that turns you on and your mind off? Except that you are not allowed to; there is no escape, not even going to the bathroom to discharge whatever it was that you ate before coming into the training.

The "no food" agreement, in conjunction with all the other agreements that you are given the "choice" to make, tends to accelerate the process through which you realize you have a mind that you have no control over, and that has absolute control over you.

The est training is a process in which you are literally driven right out of your mind, and there is nothing you can do about it except resist. (The mind's function, according to Erhard, is survival.) So the trainees often break their agreements, and some do sneak out during the bathroom break to grab something to eat, hurriedly. But it really doesn't work. It doesn't work when you eat in a hurry, and it doesn't work when you swallow broken agreements with your meal.

And again, since there are many people on this planet who have chosen not to eat for very long periods of time and never "got it," there has to be something else that makes the training work. Maybe it is the all-pervasive presence of the trainer:

> There seems to be no agent more effective than another person in bringing the world for oneself alive, or by a glance, or a gesture, or a remark shriveling up the reality in which one is lodged.
>
> —ERVING GOFFMAN
> from R.D. Laing's
> *The Politics of Experience*

The trainees' eyelids were already beginning to grow heavy. The list of agreements had been read in the same mechanical drone that had been used in countless other trainings.

"Wake up! Wake up!" shouted a voice of unknown origin in the back of the room. "Wake up!" The trainees shuddered in their seats. It was as if they had gone to bed thinking they were alone in the house, and then, as they reached over to turn out the light, the closet door opened and out stepped—

Brendan Hart, the perfect, all-American, twentieth-century samurai, and the handsomest son of a bitch I had ever seen, six foot two, with the smoothest unwrinkled flesh and features so perfect that they prompted one journalist to remark, "It was a face made out of glass and vinyl"—a face that bore no trace of a personal history, only self-confidence and power. Brendan brushed past the trainees as he moved down the center aisle toward the platform in the front of the room.

Was this a trainer, or was it an all-pro tight end currently on leave from the Denver Broncos? He walked quickly and aggressively, as if he were parading out to an athletic field knowing full well that fifty thousand spectators were watching him. Was it possible that underneath those green, gabardine slacks and the plaid sports jacket he was wearing a full uniform, right down to the jock strap and polyethylene cup? Was it the shoulder pads, the knee pads, the thigh pads, or the ankle brace that caused his apparent stiffness? Or was it that he was as uncertain as the rest of us as to what was going to happen next?

"Are you listening, people? Are you listening?" he asked. "The agreements are what this training is about. . . . They are what life is about. . . . The universe works on agreement. . . . Are you listening? The reasons why your lives don't work, the reason why you're assholes, is that you don't keep your agreements. You never listen long enough to find out what they are."

The woman sitting next to me turned to me in horror. "Is this what I paid two hundred and fifty dollars for? Is this why I gave up my first free weekend in months?" She was ready to leave, but she didn't have enough courage to move from her cocoa-colored seat.

"It ain't gonna get no better in here," Brendan snarled. "It's going to get a lot worse, and if you have any notions about not keeping your agreements, remember that you haven't got what you came here for, and I do. I've already got your two hundred and fifty bucks. I've already won.

It's going to get so bad in here that the only thing that's going to keep you in your seats is your money. Is that clear?"

It was the moment of truth, and the outraged woman sitting next to me was certainly not the only one who knew she had made a terrible mistake. There were sighs and slack-jawed disillusionment all over the training room. They were being traumatized; but this was it. This was the main event.

But as far as Brendan Hart was concerned, it was just another training in a long line of trainings that he had been giving for the last two years. He had been through six est cities in the last seven days, back and forth across the country twice to lead a special guest seminar, a pre-training, and a post-training. He had not gotten much sleep during the last week, and even though he had stood up in front of groups of people countless times before, he was nervous. The nervousness was well worked into his act in the form of that intimidating stiffness, a very subtle piece of choreography.

Brendan said that his home was in San Francisco, but he spent much of his time in airplanes, and when he wasn't registered in one of the hotels in which the trainings are given, he used planes as his bedroom. "I want to tell you something," he said. "If you think I want to be here, you're dead wrong. I'd rather be back on the beach with my wife in San Francisco."

He meant it, and he didn't. He had given up everything that is associated with having a normal life to become a trainer, but he did not particularly enjoy spending so much time away from home. There was his twenty-four-year-old wife, Becky, and his ten-month-old son, Eden.

"My wife's job is to have food in the icebox, and my clothes packed when I'm ready to go." The trouble with most people's relationships, he went on to say, is that they have too much time to spend together. "They are so bored with each other that the most interesting thing they can do is carry on." Taking a stab at the feminists in the room, "You women would be a lot happier if you realized that you get paid to clean the house and cook dinner."

"Hissssssssssssssssssssssssss, booooooooooh!" He was ruffling their feathers.

"I mean it. I don't spend a lot of time with Becky, but each time she meets me at the airport, it's like meeting a new person. Our relationship is as clean as snow. . . ." Halting his speech, Brendan lapsed into his own private space, as if he had unexpectedly re-created his wife in the training room.

Another moment went by and he was back into his act. "You assholes keep your agreements with me and your lives will work. You don't keep your agreements with me and your lives won't work. Is everybody clear on that now?"

I wasn't. I was willing to keep the agreements, but I hadn't bargained for this verbal abuse.

"Anyone who's not clear on what the agreements are around here"—softening his voice as he spoke—"this is an opportunity for you to share your consideration publicly."

I raised my hand.

"OK. Stand up and take the microphone."

In every est training there is a ritual exercise in how to hold a microphone. David Norris, the training supervisor, had put us through it earlier. "Stand up. Extend your arms. Now make a fist with your left hand around your right thumb. OK. Now with your left thumb extended outward, bring your arms back toward your mouth. All right, good. Sit down."

It was my turn. "Speaking of assholes, do you have to be one in order to deliver the training?" I stammered while I looked around for something else particularly cutting to say.

Brendan got off the platform and moved halfway up the right aisle to where I was sitting. "You worry about you. And let me worry about me. You came here to get the training. And I'm going to deliver the training the way I've been trained to deliver the training."

He walked back to the platform and leaned on the music stand that he used as a lectern. "By the way, was that a question or a statement?"

I had asked the question hoping to blow him away, but I sat down silently, feeling blown away myself. I spent the next half hour rephrasing my "statement" over and over again. I was embarrassed, and did not raise my hand again until the third day.

Brendan called on a paunchy little potato of a man in the front row. "Look," the man said, "I can go along with all these agreements. I am willing to keep my ass in the room and all that—but I'm going to ask you to guarantee us that there will be no physical violence."

"What's that?" Brendan asked, reminding him to speak into the microphone.

"I'm asking you to guarantee us that there will be no attempt to use physical violence to accomplish your objectives—no sadism, beatings, none of that," the man asked again.

A portion of the room burst into laughter, and the others seemed to take him seriously.

Provided the man kept his hands to himself, Brendan would keep his hands to himself. (I later heard of an incident involving a wrestling match between Werner Erhard and an unsatisfied graduate, but such incidents occur infrequently.)

"I can't see your name tag."

"Steve," the man said.

"Anything else, Steve?"

"One other thing. As I look around the room, I see that we are predominantly a group of middle-class whites. I don't see any blacks. I don't see any chicanos. I don't see—"

Brendan cut him off.

"My answer to your question, Steve, is that anyone can take this training. And you know something, Steve? You're the one who hates niggers."

Steve blustered, muttering caustic remarks that could not be heard.

"What's that, Steve," Brendan asked.

"Nothing," he said as he surrendered his microphone.

"One of the things you people have to get," Brendan said, "is that if you stand up and put your foot in the bear trap, you're going to get caught. It is the space that we provide for you to move through your stuff. I wish I had a formula that would make it easy, but I don't. Too bad," he said sarcastically, "too bad."

Brendan walked over to one of the two blackboards that had been placed on the left and right of the music stand and began to write down some data with a thick piece of yellow chalk.

A woman in the front row let out a "Yawwwwwn" and the room burst into laughter.

"Don't think you're going to hurt my feelings if you fall asleep. We've had people sleep through the whole training and they still got it," he said, as he continued to write down the data.

On the first day of the training we take a look at the ways through which we think we know. Rather than offer you another way of knowing, we look at how you know. We give you a chance to look through your eye with your eye, seeing what you see with what you see ... and maybe ... I'm just suggesting that what you see isn't there at all.

ROD LOGAN
at a special guest seminar

The data amounted to a simple scheme through which we were to perceive that most of what we think we know is a product of our belief systems and somebody else's options about the way the universe works.

"People hate to be in mystery about the things they don't

know . . ." Brendan said. "I mean, after all, they have a right. So they take what they don't know and they plug it into a system that we call beliefs," he went on, adding that people used to think the earth was flat.

"Any questions about what I have written up here on the board?"

The questions and answers took the form of an intellectual exercise, and it prompted all those people in the audience who thought they were intellectuals to join in. Played back over a tape recorder, it might have sounded like an introductory lecture to Aristotle's epistemology. It was being *experienced*, however, on a deeper and more subtle level.

It was not long before the trainees would be forced to eat their sacred cows, to acknowledge that what they thought they knew was only a function of what they believed.

Brendan told a story about a girl who had stood up in another training and said that she had been studying Buddhism for the last seven years, and if there was anything she believed in it was the Buddha.

"Buddha is dogshit," the trainer had said, "until you experience being the Buddha."

The girl struggled and resisted eloquently; she had seven years of her life invested in believing in the Buddha. But at a later point in the training, she stood up again and said, "Buddha is dogshit." It was your typical Zen story. "At that point she received enlightenment," Brendan told us.

"Don't transform the beliefs," Erhard says, "transform the believer." It wasn't so much that Buddha was dogshit; it was that, according to Erhard, the truth believed—even the Buddha's truth—is a lie. It is the *experience* of the truth—the experience of not having that little voice in the back of your head telling you that if you believe in the Buddha "your ass will be saved"—that creates the space for people to get in touch with the Buddha that is within them.

"You already were saved," Brendan shouted, quoting Erhard, "and this is the way it turned out!" He began to wrap up the discussion on "knowing" by asking us why our arms moved when we raised them. "Anybody know? Anyone?"

Hands were raised.

"Wilma?" He called on a tall woman in the back row.

"The muscles contract," Wilma said.

"They do, huh?" Brendan asked. "What makes them contract? Somebody else? . . . OK, Richard, stand up and take a microphone."

"They receive a stimulus from the brain."

"Wait a minute," Brendan said. "How do you know you have a brain?"

There was a pause. "Because that's the way we came into this universe," Richard replied.

"What universe?"

Richard sat down.

"You people don't know anything, do you? Do you?"

The walls of the room began to close in around me and I drifted off into an experience I once had in the Park Street subway station in Boston. I was leaning against a concrete pole and trying to look at people's auras.

The technique is presumably simple: Unfocus your eyes, look at the space around the person, not directly at him, and with any luck, you will be able to see a transparent envelope of energy pulsating around the tip of the nose, the forehead, the temples. I had learned the technique from John Pierakos, a bioenergy specialist in New York who uses it to diagnose energy blockages in his patients. Simple enough for John Pierakos, it was nonetheless very difficult for me to put into practice with any degree of success.

I looked from person to person in the precariously lit subway as if I were looking into a cloud; and then my eyes caught a glimpse of a billboard advertising the Massachusetts State Lottery. I had been able to see only the vague outlines of people's faces, but the instant I looked at that sign my eyes were riveted into absolute attention. It was a moment of revelation for me, in which all my years of education shot through my mind like an express train.

All I could see was print—linear train tracks of type.

I understood at that point that all I had learned in my years of education was to screen out a whole universe of invisible energy. I looked away from the billboard in a sudden realization of my own absolute ignorance; and then came the unexpected, the aura: the blues, greens, whites, golds of at least a hundred people standing in the dimly lit subway station.

I later wrote about this experience in an article entitled "The School of the Ignoramus." (*East West Journal*, September 1974.) In that piece I noted, "Whoever said ignorance was bliss was right," meaning that as you begin to get in touch with your own ignorance, you also begin to ignore the linearity of your previous world of perception.

It was as if I had suddenly been transported into another dimension of being. In that state, I was able to look at my experience with a childlike sense of wonder, and to know that I did not know.

"And when you know that you don't know," Brendan said, "that's the beginning of knowing."

It seemed as if I had been away from the room for more than a half hour, but at that point I began to wake up to the est training. It was not that I had learned something new. It was that the training had put me in touch with what I already knew.

That is the way the training works. It had re-created an experience in me that was too powerful to deny.

"All right," Brendan said, "we're going to do a process in a few minutes, but I'm going to read you what G. Spencer Brown had to say about the natural mind first." He picked up his notebook from the music stand and began to read, as if he were telling us a bedtime story about a philosopher fool, stopping occasionally to simplify the vocabulary.

"It is often forgotten that the ancient symbol of prenascence [before the birth of the world] is a fool, and that foolishness being a divine state is not a condition to be either proud or ashamed of . . ."

"Now, when I say 'divine,' please don't attach any religious significance to it . . . he means it in terms of the creative divine," he said, interrupting himself.

"Unfortunately, the methods of education today have departed so far from the plain truth that it now teaches us to be proud of what we know and ashamed of ignorance. This is doubly corrupt . . ."

"Now you want to be very clear about the words here . . . and if you look corrupt up, it means wrongdoing," he said, interrupting himself again.

"All right," Brendan said. "Close your eyes, sit up straight, and take everything off your laps. . . .

"Get in touch with a space in your left foot," Brendan directed us. "All right. . . . Get in touch with a space in your right foot. . . . good. . . . Get in touch with a space in your left ankle. . . . Thank you. . . . Locate a space in your right ankle. . . . Good. . . . Get in touch with a space inside your left knee. . . . All right; good." He went on and on like that until he was certain that we were fully in touch with our bodies.

Although processes are also referred to in est as "directed meditation," there are no sacred mantras or trappings of any kind. A process is simply a space provided in the training where you can be alone with yourself and whatever is going on with you. It is not uncommon in the training for the trainer to say something that sets off a series of psychological chain reactions in you that you cannot deal with fully, given all the stimuli in the room. When you are alone in a process, you are provided with an opportunity to watch the scenarios as they go by. It may be the same old stuff (an unsatisfactory relationship, for example), but you often see it in a different way, as if someone had suddenly shifted the camera angle and allowed you a glimpse of things as they are.

Sometimes all of that happens, and sometimes it doesn't. I was so hungry and I had to go to the bathroom so badly during the first process that by the time the trainer said "Get in touch with a space between your groin and your rectum," I was ready to wet my pants. I was bored, tired, and squirming in my seat—no chain reactions—nothing to think about except the growing agony that I was experiencing with each passing moment.

"Begin to re-create the space of the room," Brendan said. "I'm going to count backwards from ten, and when I reach one, you can open your eyes: Ten . . . nine . . . eight . . . seven . . . six . . . five . . . four . . . three . . . two . . . one. . . . OK, you can open your eyes."

I sighed in relief.

Brendan asked us to share what went on with us during the process, and then said "We're going to take a break."

David Norris walked down the center aisle to join Brendan on the platform. "This is not a meal break," David said, as he began to give precise instructions as to the location of the bathrooms. "It is now three o'clock. . . ."

Amazed that they had been in the room so long, the trainees clamored in unison. "Ouuuuuu," as the absence of time pieces began to make sense.

"The break will last thirty-five minutes," David said. "Be back in your seats by three thirty-five."

The trainees filed out of Conference Room A like a herd of stampeding elephants.

I don't know what was going on in the ladies' room, but in the men's room, except for a few cases of "pee lock," the urine flowed like Lake Erie spilling over Niagara Falls. The scent of urine drifted into the coffee shop, and I was still aware of it when I reached the bank of elevators that were already taking people back up to the sixth floor.

There were so many people waiting to use the bathroom next to the coffee shop that I didn't get a chance to go. So as soon as the elevator stopped, I scurried over to the sixth floor men's room, reaching nirvana. Oh, heavenly ecstasy, the moment that I pulled the cork!

"Back into your seats," shouted an est assistant through the bathroom door. "We're about to begin." Back in my seat I couldn't think of anything but food. I spent the next three hours totally unconscious of what was going on in the room and dreaming about all the things I never allow myself to eat. (I have been a quasi vegetarian for sometime.)

I left the conference room firmly resolved to eat anything that didn't crawl during the meal break, which was called at nine P.M. It was to last an hour and a half. I wandered down to the Golden Gate restaurant in Boston's Chinatown and ordered the works. Peking ravioli, wonton soup, Moo Shi pork, and the Vegetarian's Delight. I ate so much and so fast that after tossing down a couple of fortune cookies, I found it difficult to walk back to the conference room.

I lumbered through the Combat Zone and arrived at the hotel coffee shop at around ten o'clock. I sat down next to a friend and ordered a cup of tea with lemon.

Prior to the meal break I had not talked to anyone in over twelve hours. I had sat with utter passivity in the conference room, soaking up data as a fuel-injected carburetor soaks up gasoline. By the time the meal break was called, my psychic engines were revved up to the maximum as a result of all the internal combustion that was going on in my mind. I had looked forward to testing my wheels on the open road, but I had wound up eating dinner alone.

The food had animated me; and not long after my friend and I began our conversation I felt myself tooling down a psychic superhighway, with pieces of data breezing past and vanishing like road signs seen in a rearview mirror.

My friend suggested that instead of returning to the training room we go over to the Seventh Inn, a natural foods restaurant that serves the best strawberry shortcake in town, and continue our conversation.

I was a bit taken aback, but it was either that or go back to revving my engines in the passivity of the conference room, which at this point was about as appealing to me as a garage. I hit the suggestion like a patch of grease on a sharp-winding mountain road.

I skidded off the mountain and did not return to the conference room until the following morning.

Chapter IV
WHAT YOU RESIST, PERSISTS

The first day of the training had ended at about three o'clock in the morning with a lesson in how to get up in the morning awake and aware without an alarm clock. The trainees were back in their seats by nine A.M., surprisingly refreshed and ready to begin. For many it was a vivid demonstration that they really didn't need eight or nine hours of sleep, they only believed they did. For many others it was a realization that even a lesson well-learned does not work all the time, which began to fill them with doubts about the training itself.

Brendan walked down the center aisle as if he had stepped out of the tub only a minute ago, and received a bursting shower of applause. "Good morning!" Even though the trainees spoke through a microphone, the trainer's unassisted voice was always three or four decibels louder than theirs.

"Good morning!" the trainees bellowed back.

"Today we are going to take a look at a thing we call experience," Brendan said. "We're going to take it apart and put it back together again with the intention of expanding your ability to experience living."

Recapping the purpose of the est training, which is "to

expand your ability to experience living so that the situations you have been trying to change or have been putting up with begin to clear up just in the process of life itself," he began to construct an analogy comparing experience to "Grandma's Vermont stew."

"Experience is like a Vermont stew; and if you know anything about stew, you know that it contains a whole list of ingredients. It's got onions. It's got carrots. It's got potatoes. It's got everything that goes into a stew; and you put that all into a caldron, add some water, and out comes old Grandma's favorite recipe.

"What I'm going to ask you to do is to get in touch with one item in the stew we call your experience, one that is particularly real for you. Is it a body sensation? Is it an emotion? Is it an attitude toward life? Which one of these will you use as your item in a process we are going to do later in the day?"

I chose "vital shock," the implosion of body sensations one gets when he sees a hockey puck or a baseball flying toward his gut at a hundred miles an hour. (One can substitute a pink slip in one's paycheck for the baseball, or the loss of a government contract for the hard-hitting puck.) I had only to think about it to begin to feel my stomach dropping and my mind freezing up in a singular contortion of panic.

"Be as specific as possible," Brendan went on, "and be careful not to assign a cause to your item." Using the analogy of the stew again: "Remember, a carrot doesn't cause a potato, nor does a pea cause an onion."

I took this to mean that I was to concentrate on the sensation, not the apparent "cause"—the hockey puck or the baseball.

"What we are going to do today is get as close as we can to factoring out what is in the recipe. And if you look at your experience, you'll see that it is made up of three basic ingredients.

"It's got the fact that it exists—the abstract. It's got the substance—the construct (it may be fear). And it's got a context—the stew. I'm going to ask you to let go of the abstract and the construct, so you can grab hold of the substance of the experience—a pea, a potato, or whatever it is that you choose."

I was somewhat confused.

"It may be a sharp pain, the size of a quarter, behind my right eye," he went on, "or it may be a dull, aching sensation, the size of a grapefruit, below my breastbone; or it may be an emotion that I don't seem to have any control over."

We were not asked to choose our "most significant" item. Brendan said that by choosing an item now that was right on the surface, we would later be able to dig in and grab the significant one—the one we had been reaching for. We were then told to take our fingers off the "repress button."

"Allow it to boil up in you. Allow it to take command. Allow it to control you, instead of your trying to control it." Brendan emphasized that we were to submit ourselves totally to our items; this would allow us to "experience them out" in the "truth process" that we would do later.

"If you look at anything long enough," he said, "and tell the truth about it, it will disappear. It will literally disappear."

I wasn't sure what he meant.

"I mean you will not have it anymore."

I assumed that we would be shortly led into the process, but there were many trainees who had not yet selected their items. Brendan began a period of "sharing" with the trainees, using some new data he had scrawled on the blackboard as a context to assist them in their sharing.

The process was to last eleven hours! "What you resist experiencing, persists," he said. "It runs you like a machine."

It began to occur to me that the training, including the abusive language of the trainer, was intentionally designed to activate our resistance; and even when there was little or no resistance left, the trainer would press on.

"Press your buttons and you'll go off like a machine. . . . A machine has no choice in the way it acts. It is wired up in such a way that all you have to do is press its buttons, and you'll start dumping like the mechanical assholes that you are," Brendan said.

A woman named Mary interrupted him, "It's not necessary to use that kind of language," she said, smiling at him pertly.

"Oh," he said imitating her, "it isn't necessary to use that kind of language. I got that, Mary, so you can wipe that sexy little smile off your face. I want you to notice Mary's act: Press her buttons and she smiles.

"You've been smiling all your life, Mary, and where has it gotten you? Right here!"

She started to whimper.

"Press another button and Mary starts to cry. Press another button and she screws. . . . Mary, you ain't nothin' but a little china doll. Do you get that? Thank you, Mary, you can sit down. . . .

"I was only using Mary as an example," he said. "There isn't one person in here that I couldn't manipulate as easily as I manipulated Mary.

"I'm gonna assist you in choosing your item, but play me any of those tapes about being the victim, and you'll wind up with your foot in the bear trap.

"OK, raise your hand if you want to share."

Hands were raised, and Brendan began the seemingly endless period of sharing.

"OK, John. Stand up and take a microphone."

"I'm experiencing not resisting anymore. I'm experiencing being my bladder, and having a wet spot that runs from my groin to the bottom of my pants."

Laughter.

"John's experiencing being the effect of having to go to the bathroom, and by the way, if any of you want to wet your pants, you don't have my permission. Have you found your item yet?"

"Embarrassment," John said.

"Embarrassment is a concept," Brendan replied.
"Guilt."
"Guilt is a concept. . . . Pick an item, any item."
"Fear . . . sadness . . ." John was caught between the two.
"Pick one," Brendan said.
"Fear."
"All right, fear. Good, John, sit down."

        clapclapclapclapclapclapclapclapclap
              clapclapclapclapclapclapclap
                    clapclapclap

"Susan. . . ." He pointed her out to the person with the microphone. "Over here."

"My item is," Susan said, "that I can't stand living with my mother. She's eighty years old and she wants me to stay home every night and entertain her. . . . Let's see, what else? She listens to my phone calls on the extension, and . . . I would have moved out of the house by now, but I feel sorry for her. She's—"

"Yammayammayammayamma—that's a lot of horseshit, Susan. I'm asking you to select an item."

"Hate."

"Hate is a concept," he said.

"You don't know my mother. She's—"

"What you gotta get, Susan, is that you set it up to have a mother like that. You created it, and now you don't want to take responsibility for dealing with it," Brendan said.

"What do you mean, I created it? She's—"

"Another thing you people want to get is that I mean exactly what I say. I mean you created it, and you don't want to take responsibility for the way it is with you and your mother." He continued to bear down on her. "Have you told your mother about the way you feel about her?"

"I couldn't do that. It would kill her," she said, staring back at him in horror.

He was setting her up, the same way he had set Mary up,

and the same way he would set up dozens of other people during the rest of the day. Setting her up for what? Exactly what he said, to acknowledge that she was the cause of her own experience and that she must take responsibility for it. Responsibility? Brendan said it began with a simple acceptance that you are at cause in a situation; adding that it did not imply "praise, blame, shame, or guilt," as these often involve negative judgments that go beyond a simple acknowledgment that you created a situation the way it is.

"If you're not the cause of your own experience with your mother, who is? Who is?" He had baited the trap and she was about to fall in. "You don't care if your mother lives or dies, do you?"

She started to whimper. "No . . . I don't," she said as she broke down completely.

"What are you experiencing right now?" he asked.

"Anger." There was a pause; "I feel very angry."

"Are you willing to choose anger as your item?" he asked.

"Yes."

"One more thing . . . Are you willing to re-create your mother so that you can live with her?" he asked sympathetically.

"Yes, I love her," she said.

"I know you love her . . . Stick around. And you'll have a chance to do that during the second weekend of the training.

"Thank you, Susan. You can sit down," he said.

clapclapclapclapclapclapclapclapclapclap
clapclapclapclap
clapclap

"I want to acknowledge Susan for having the courage to stand up in front of two hundred and fifty people and share that," Brendan said gently.

clapclapclapclapclapclapclapclap
clapclapclapclapclapclap
clapclapclap

"OK, James. What's your item?"

"Whenever I get around my boss, I feel like he's going to fire me."

"*How* do you feel when you're around your boss?" Brendan interrupted, throwing the question back in his lap. "Be specific!"

"I feel nervous," James said.

"Any body sensations associated with that?"

"My hands get hot . . . and I feel a lightness here," James said, pointing to an area below his rib cage.

"Good enough," Brendan said.

clapclapclapclap
clapclapclap

One of the most revealing aspects of the training is how close to the surface the things we try to hide from ourselves are. The further back these things go in our experience, the more powerful the effect they have on our present patterns of behavior and attitudes towards life.

"Have you selected an item yet, Cheryl?" Brendan called on a tall, wavy-haired woman who wore wire-rim glasses.

"When you were taking us through the last process and you said to locate a space inside our stomachs. I— I—" Cheryl's arms went up around her head and she stood there weeping. "What I started to say—"

Brendan raced down the right aisle. "OK, Cheryl, what do you see?"

"A white room—" Half a breath at a time.

"A white room," Brendan repeated, "Now what's going on inside the white room?"

"Bright lights," she said. "Everyone is dressed in white—" (Sob!) "It's got to be a hospital." Cheryl had been in a hospital only twice in her life, once to get her tonsils taken out and—

"What's going on in the white room that you say is a hospital?" Brendan asked again.

"I'm being born," she said, gasping for breath between her sobs.

"What are you experiencing right now, Cheryl? What are you experiencing right now?" Brendan prodded.

"That my mother doesn't love me," she moaned, "that she doesn't want me to be born."

It was as if the delivery were taking place in Conference Room A. It was.

I couldn't believe that what was going on in the room was actually going on; nor could I believe that the est training was this powerful. I was able to get in touch with my own very deep sadness as Cheryl continued to speak.

"What are you doing now, Cheryl?" Brendan asked.

"I'm holding my breath and turning blue," she stammered.

Pulling her out to the aisle, Brendan said, "I want you all to take a look and see what Cheryl is wearing today."

She was dressed in a blue work shirt, dark-blue cotton pants, and powder-blue tennis shoes.

"She's a blue baby," he said.

The trainees broke into laughter.

"You're laughing, and she's been miserable ever since she was born. Shows you the kind of people you are," Brendan chided.

He sent her back to her seat. "All right, Cheryl. Were there any decisions you made at that time?"

She was surprisingly candid about them. "I decided that I was going to be a failure—" gasp! "—that I was going—"

She started crying again.

"Another one was that I was never going to communicate with other people—that I wouldn't be a woman—that I would only breathe enough to stay alive—and that I would live to be a hundred," she said, lighting up.

I later had an opportunity to ask Cheryl how she felt as Brendan hovered over her, prodding her with questions. "I felt good about it," she said. "I felt safe."

"OK, Cheryl, have you found your item?" Brendan asked.

"Yes."

"That's fabulous, Cheryl. Thank you very, very much."

clapclapclapclapclapclapclapclap
clapclapclapclapclap
clapclap

In the hours that followed, we would hear at least forty other people share their items.

Intending to speed things up, Brendan told us to get in touch with an item in our experience that we were either ashamed of or didn't want other people to find out about.

One Irish woman admitted to being so depressed that she was near suicide, and a young man dressed in a bright-green rayon leisure suit admitted to being a closet homosexual.

"Listen," Brendan intoned, "there isn't a person in this room who hasn't been afraid that he was a homosexual. The difference is that most of us have denied the experience because we were afraid someone would find out."

And on, and on. . . . Bernie, a middle-aged man in the front row center, stood up and said he was a shoplifter. He had tried to stop, but ...

"Bernie, I'll bet you steal because it's exciting, don't you? And you probably wouldn't steal anymore if you found something else that was just as exciting. Would you?

"I'm not saying it's wrong to steal," Brendan went on, "but it isn't appropriate. In this society stealing doesn't work; besides which, the human mind is so ethical that it will always set the thief up to be caught. Now, to steal with a free mind, that might be different."

Would it? I asked myself.

"There's no one who can be ripped off unless he wants to

be," Brendan added as Bernie found his item and returned to his seat.

"By the way," Brendan said, turning to the rest of us, "there's no difference between the rest of you and someone like Bernie. I know you steal. I know you robbed your mother's pocketbook, and you cheat on your income taxes and go through red lights and don't pay your parking tickets. It's the same thing. Stealing!"

I closed my eyes to rest them from the glare of the fluorescent lighting. I had a vision in which I was looking into the rear view mirror of my car. There was a state trooper following me, and the bubble-gum machine on top of his patrol car was flashing blue light into the darkness.

Not long thereafter, Brendan called a bathroom break.

David Norris, the training supervisor, returned to the platform carrying a piece of yellow notebook paper. "Will the following people see me before the end of the break? Stanton Becker, Lester Hinds, Emma Nataupsky, George Simmons, Nancy Michelson, and Robert Hargrove."

That was my name at the tail end of the list. Vital shock. I could already feel my stomach dropping. What did he want to talk to me about? Had somebody told him I had left early the night before? I ran down the right aisle pushing people aside and caught David before he stepped off the platform.

"I'm Robert Hargrove." The words slipped out of my mouth slowly, as if I were mouthing somebody else's name.

David drew me aside. He looked deeply into my eyes and then turned his head away. He opened his mouth and closed it again.

Was he feeling compassion for me?

He looked into my eyes again and said, "You didn't come back after the meal break last night, did you?"

"No." I told him, "with good reason." But he knew I was lying through my teeth. My hands were hot and sweaty.

"All right. I'm going to have to speak to Brendan," he said. "See me at the end of the break."

I spent the break wandering around the hotel as if I had received a phone call informing me that someone very close to me had died. I didn't know what to say or do about it. I stared blankly; and when people tried to talk to me, I said nothing and looked away, as if somewhere—on the tips of their shoes or on the red vinyl walls of the men's room—I had discovered the key to the whole universe.

I could feel the corners of my mouth turn uncontrollably into a paralyzed expression of sadness. How did they catch me? I asked myself. Was it a mystical occurrence of some kind? And then I realized I had not turned in my name tag the night before. They must have checked them against the registration cards. But why had they waited this long to tell me? It was five o'clock. My panic heightened. Were they going to throw me out of the training? Would they let me take it again?

Badgered by these questions, I rushed back into the training room several minutes early, and saw David Norris sitting at a long table in the back of the room.

As in a huddled ritual between the son of a mafia don and a not-so-trusty lieutenant, we began our conversation.

"Did you speak to Brendan?" I asked.

"I did," he said—and nothing more.

"What did he say?" I asked waiting for the world to cave in.

"He said that you may complete the training, but if you do this again, that's the end of it," David replied.

"The end of it!" The last time Brendan had used those words, it was in reference to a pine box.

David drew closer to me and stared penetratingly into my eyes again.

"Did you break your agreement?" he asked.

"Yes, I broke my agreement." I winced at a stabbing pain in the back of my head.

"Do you know that what you did is completely against the ground rules of this training?" he asked again.

"I do."

"Are you willing to be responsible for breaking your agreement?"

"I am." I was impaled by the question.

"Are you willing to remake your agreement?" he asked.

"I am." Was I being let off the hook?

"Thank you," he said. "You may take a seat now."

So I began to relax.

There were still more than a dozen people who hadn't selected their items yet, and the sharing continued.

People were talking about the deepest and darkest secrets in their lives, but somehow the atmosphere seemed less heavy—as if the sharing had somehow released their burden of guilt. It was not long before that anything anyone said began to seem funny, and the trainees began to laugh hysterically.

The sharing seemed to have a subliminal effect; and I began to realize that there wasn't anything anyone else had experienced or been afraid to experience that I hadn't experienced myself on some level: fear, anger, sadness, the trauma of childbirth, homosexuality, stealing, and suicide—the list could go on indefinitely.

Brendan called on a man wearing a bright-yellow sweater and turquoise necklace. "Tom. Stand up and take the microphone."

"I'm a little confused. When you say whatever we've been holding onto is going to disappear in the process, could that mean happiness? I guess I'm resisting choosing my item because I . . . Do you see what I mean?" he asked humbly.

"I've got that, Tom," Brendan said, "and if you can't accept the truth—if you can't be with things that are bad in your life—what that means is that your life is run on the consideration that whatever you think is good is going to turn bad. Thank you for sharing that, Tom," he said turning to the rest of us again.

"If you're holding onto something, if you've got something special tucked away in a little silver box, I want you to know that the next time you open that box you're going to find a pile of crap. Anything held onto eventually turns to dross. It turns to worthlessness!"

Someone asked a question about things disappearing.

Brendan picked up two pieces of chalk and said, "Imagine that you have two pieces of chalk in each hand . . . Now bring them together so that they both occupy the same space. What happens?"

"They disappear," shouted the trainees.

"I know it's difficult for the mind to get—it's not figure-out-able—but two objects cannot occupy the same space," he said. "In the truth process that we're going to be doing now, I'm going to ask you to re-create your experience by getting in touch with your item.

"I want to tell you, that process is so powerful that your life is going to be turned around one hundred and eighty degrees."

We were then told to stack our chairs in the back of the room. It would be a long process, and we would do it lying down on the red-carpeted floor. We were all in "mystery" suspense. It had taken all day to get to this dramatic turning point in the training and we wondered what was going to happen next.

I began to get in touch with my item during the truth process as soon as Brendan told us again to "take our fingers off the repress button" and "allow the stuff to come up." Remembering that what you resist you become, I allowed my mind to wander into the experiences I had earlier as a result of leaving the room yesterday. And it was not long before I began to associate my item with every broken agreement in my life. It wasn't a conceptual realization. I was literally re-experiencing things that had happened to me in the distant past as if they were taking place in present time. Vital shock. I was right in the midst of it, and yet I could begin to feel that sense of contraction, that claw-hold in my gut, release its grip.

"If your item has disappeared, you can go to the beach

and play," Brendan said, meaning that we could relax and imagine that we were lying on our favorite beaches, listening to the music of the sea.

I was not ready to go to the beach, but I was relaxed enough to listen to the music in the room. "Ohhhhhhhhhhh! Ahhhhhhhhhhhhh!" "Why didn't you tell me?" "Ouuuuuu- uuuuuuu!" There were deep moans and hollow groans as more and more people took their fingers off the repress button and allowed their stuff to come up. It was like listening to a secret sound track of Dante's *Inferno*—as if someone had plugged an audio hookup into the purgatorial paintings of Hieronymus Bosch.

The noise seemed to accelerate the process itself as almost everyone in the room began to let go:

"Huhahuhahuhahuhahuhahuha," breathless,
   "Oh, Goddddddd," like incantations
      of "sighhhhhhhhhhing," forgotten experience
         re-created, then disappearing.

Brendan ended the process by telling us to "re-create the room." "I'm going to count backwards from ten, and when I reach five, you can open your eyes: Ten . . . nine . . . eight . . . seven . . . six . . . five, four, three, two, one. . . . OK, open your eyes and come out of your space."

We spent a while sharing what we had experienced and Brendan called a meal break. "Stay with it during the meal break," he said. "Don't go unconscious."

I spent the meal break with friends, sharing my experience as Brendan had told us to do. I did not have any thoughts of leaving early, and I was back in the training room with more than fifteen minutes to spare. I was ready to take part in the "danger process" that would follow. I noticed that the chairs had been moved back into long, straight rows.

The danger process took place in two parts; the first part we would do in our chairs, and the second in prone position again. It was supposed to deal with what is between us and being with other people.

I will not go into detail here as I have an agreement not to. I have however created a little process of my own that may put you in touch with the kind of things that come up in the first part of the process. It is *not* intended as a substitute for the actual experience.

Get in touch with an experience you've had when you had to look into the eyes of someone you've had trouble communicating with.

... OK

Get in touch with an experience you've had when it was necessary to break the ice with someone you didn't like.

all right ...

Get in touch with an experience you've had when you were first afraid you were a homosexual.

... fine

Get in touch with an experience you've had when a beggar asked you for some money.

good ...

Get in touch with an experience you've had when you wanted to tell somebody you loved them, and were afraid or embarrassed to.

... all right

Imagine a time that you felt lonely.

OK ...

Imagine that you are talking to someone you know. Move your left hand with your fingers spread apart toward the area of your face—keeping in mind that you are still talking to someone you know. Move your left hand across your eyes and face (fingers spread). Do this again, only this time imagine that the movement of your hand is a thought. Experience being away from the person you are talking to. Repeat this process, only this time with your fingers not spread apart, imagining the movement of your hand to be an evaluation of the person you are talking to.

. . . .

Imagine that the person you are talking to is doing the same thing at the same time.

. . . .

Imagine two tape recorders talking to each other.

. . . .

Turn the play button off and imagine that you are in danger.

P. D. Ouspensky, a student of G. I. Gurdjieff, once wrote, "If a man would work on himself, he must be prepared to lose his peace." It is an apt metaphor for the est training and particularly the second part of the danger process.

In agreeing to be in the training, it was not the intention of the trainees to lose their peace, but by the end of the truth process they were well-prepared to, even if it meant walking through an imaginary minefield with their eyes closed, or being trapped in an elevator with the Boston Strangler.

"Want to see how dangerous you can be?" we were asked by the trainer the following weekend. "Walk into a dimly lit bar on Saturday night when everyone is supposed to be having a good time," he continued. "Turn on the lights and look a couple of people in the eye."

This implied too much danger to be taken seriously, but lying on the floor with my eyes closed, I could feel shuddering bodies all around me, and I could hear shrieking cries for help.

Were these people being tortured by a master of the Spanish Inquisition, or by their own fear?

Since I could not feel the point of a knife blade at my throat, or a red-hot coal in my mouth, I knew that whatever I was afraid of had to be imaginary.

And was this process any less real than life?

Was it any different from walking through the Combat Zone at night?

Was it any different from walking into the boss's office knowing that he is going to fire you?

Was it any different from walking past a barking dog?

Toward the end of the process, I recalled something that Ram Dass had written in *Be Here Now:*

It's the vibrations that emanate from you.

If your vibrations are paranoid,
    that's what's being received.

And when you're around pets,
    (birds or cats particularly)
    or very young children,
    or very flipped-out psychotics,

They will know you immediately.

And you can come and say,
    "Hello, dear, how are you?"

And the dog will growl ...

You can't come on,
    because they're listening.

And when you realize that you'll know,
    that at every moment,
    you are a full statement of your being,
    sending out vibrations
    that are affecting everything around you,
    which in turn is affecting everything
    that comes back.

It all comes back to this: What you resist, persists.
If you resist any item in your experience (including people) you will be in fear.
If you resist fear, you will be in danger.
(You will be bitten by dogs.)
I opened my eyes toward the very end of the process, and I saw the person lying next to me.
She had a serene expression on her madonna face.
I closed my eyes again and heard chortling and laughter.
Even danger produces its opposite at its extreme.
I experienced the "safe space" of the training room for the first time.
"Open your eyes and come out of your space." Brendan ended the evening by telling us to walk up to someone we didn't know during the next week and say, "Booooooo!"
He stood by the doors grinning like a Cheshire cat, shaking hands with the graduates as they left the training room.
"Thank you very much, Brendan," I said, moving close to him.
"Hey, come here," he said, putting his arms around me. "Thank you."

Chapter V

OUT THERE IN THE ILLUSION

The days between the first and second weekends of the training passed as if in a single night, during which I would wake up often in a state of realization and then go back to sleep in the warm bed of my unconsciousness.

It was as if the earth had suddenly shifted its axis and my whole way of looking at the world had been turned upside down.

I saw myself being swept from the stagnant pool of my previous models of perception and drawn into the river of conscious life.

The training was like a power in me, sometimes an active volcano bringing up stuff like molten lava, and at other times a hibernating bear. "Whackkkk!" Caught my foot in the bear trap—the crush of reality's sharp teeth as I allowed myself to play the impotent victim, at the level of effect.

I rode up and down on the est roller coaster.

I was exactly the same, and like the graduate at the post-training, totally different: happy/unhappy, open/closed, afraid/unafraid, terribly foolish/infinitely wise. It was not understandable, it was only (as they say in est) "experienceable," and I began to accept it as "what's so."

I spent a good part of the week working in my vegetable garden; and it wasn't long before I noticed that whenever anything went wrong (such as peas not coming up) I looked around for somebody else to blame—except that there was nobody else out there. I began to "get" that I almost always blamed other people for things that went wrong; it was a way of avoiding responsibility. I got angry every time the hose failed to reach my squash plants, but each time I *noticed* that I was experiencing anger, and that I had "considerations" about hoses. It seemed like a small realization at first, but by the middle of the week, it began to extend into my relationships with other people. I was able to come from "cause" in my relationships; and when something went wrong I would not attribute to other people the emotions I was experiencing.

I would ask myself, "Why isn't she out there helping me in the garden?" and then stop to think, "Why aren't you out there, when you're out there in the garden?"

By the end of the week, I was able to work in the garden with my anger, and not be run by it. I was able to do whatever I had set out to do by letting go of all the effort I was putting into my "considerations" about other people's not helping me. By acknowledging whatever "came up" while I was working, whether it was body sensation, emotion, thought, consideration, or image from the past, I began to experience what "acceptance" was.

This is the initial step "above the line" of satisfaction. In being able to accept that things are the way they are—and not the way they are not—I was able to work in the garden, and in my relationships, with the satisfaction that I brought *to* them and without seeking the satisfaction I had previously been seeking *from* them. It seemed like a miracle, but I did begin to experience my life's being "turned around one hundred and eighty degrees." And then the whole thing would turn around again, and I would be back in my original position—the victim, totally affected by whatever was going on around me.

"The Kingdom of Heaven is within you." How many times had I heard that cosmic joke before? I had interviewed about every swami, guru, mahatma, and rinpoche that had come to America, but no one had been able to tell it to me in a way that I could "get it." "The Kingdom of Heaven is within you." It had been rephrased and restated in every quasi-religious trip that had come along since Maharishi began stocking the shelves of America's spiritual supermarket with Transcendental Meditation. And the more times I heard it, the more of a meaningless cliché it became. Was I to find it within me?

"Getting it," Brendan had said, "We all would."

And I went into the second weekend of the training wondering whether or not I would finally see the light at the end of the long tunnel of psycho-spiritual, self-development trips I had been through.

On the third day of the training, David Norris strolled up the center aisle like a proud Bar Mitzvah boy with a large rump.

Until now his verbal communication with the trainees had been limited to his mechanical recitation of the list of agreements, in addition to precise instructions as to the location of the bathrooms and nearby restaurants. But now there was another level of communication taking place. It was David's *presence* in the training room, and his ability to see that there were no interruptions of any kind, that seemed to make it a "safe space" for people to share. In handling all the humdrum details of managing the training, David seemed to make it possible for the trainer to handle whatever else came up.

Webster's gives one definition of *presence* as "an influence of a supernatural or *divine spirit felt to be present*." It is as close as I can come to re-creating David's presence in the training room.

David reached the platform, and the trainees greeted him with their previously unacknowledged gratitude.

clapclapclapclapclapclap
clapclapclapclapclap
clapclap

"Thank you. We're going to start by giving you a chance to share what's been going on since last weekend," David said. He then turned the floor over to the trainees, listening attentively and without comment as each one spoke.

It was much like the sharing that took place at the post-training: One person would stand up and say, "I've had the best week in my entire existence," and another would counter with, "It's been so horrible, I—" It was a cross between a Southern Baptist revival meeting and a public confessional—no music, but a comparable profusion of emotion.

When most people hear the word "sharing," they think of a time when they were children, a time when somebody told them to share, and instead of having a whole candy bar, they had only half. In est sharing is a willingness to acknowledge "what is" (the situation as it is) "without running your number" (complaining). Although numbers are often endured, they are seldom tolerated for very long.

"Thirty seconds!" shouted an est staff assistant every time a person reached the minute-and-a-half mark. "Please limit your sharing to two minutes."

"Time's up!"

An acknowledgment of *what is* is a transitional step toward acceptance, which is what "getting it" is all about.

Although sharing is not required in the est training, almost everyone rises to do it by the third day; and anyone who has not had a chance to share in any given part of the training is asked to do so—along with everyone else—in something called "paired sharing."

"All right," David called out. "Turn to the person sitting next to you. Everybody get a partner. . . . The person with the lightest hair is A. All right, Bs, you have three minutes to share whatever's been going on with you." And the As would follow.

After the paired sharing was over, David introduced Rod Logan, who was to be our trainer for the second weekend.

```
clapclapclapclapclapclapclap
                  clapclapclapclapclap
             clapclapclap
        clapclap
             clapclap
```

Rod walked down the center toward the platform, and said, in a much deeper voice than Brendan's, "Helloooooooooo."

The trainees, who had been trained in saying hello the previous weekend, shot back, "Hellooooooooooooooooooooooo," with considerable bravado.

Rod smiled, "That's not bad, but let's have it again: Helloooooooooooooooooooo."

"Helloooooooooooooooooooooooooooooooooooooooo."

The trainees returned the greeting with booming amplification. Its effect was instantaneous, and I thought of all the times I had looked at people's shoes or over their heads while shaking their hands or meeting them. In that simple greeting was a new certainty that I was unaccustomed to.

"That's more like it," said Rod, and we were off to a flying start.

My first reaction to Rod was that he wasn't as handsome as Brendan. Not that he wasn't good-looking. He carried himself with a sense of grace and an air of sophistication that went well with the role he was about to play. Rod's face was shaped like an ax, and his features reminded me of a statue I had once seen of Sophocles. He wore a perfectly fitting pair of beige polyester pants and a silver-gray sport shirt, with epaulets, that matched his steel-gray hair.

I spent the first half hour or so dealing with my attachment to Brendan, and before long I began to see why the trainings were set up so that whoever was the trainer on the first weekend wasn't the trainer on the second. The experience of training was so powerful that it would be easy to associate it with the presence of a particular trainer. I considered all the people I had known who had had powerful experiences with a Guru Great or a Swami Anybodyananda—people who never seemed to be happy unless they were in the personal presence of the Dharma heavy himself. They were so hung up on the guru that they forgot what he was saying: "The experience is within you."

I began to realize why most of the trainers looked and dressed alike. It made them invisible, and although this annoyed certain journalists because it seemed to wash out any clue to their personal history, it nonetheless seemed to achieve the desired result. Within an hour after Rod was introduced, it became very difficult to discern any difference between him and Brendan. He was "the trainer," delivering the training, the way he had been trained to deliver the training, and that was all. If there had been a robot up there instead of Rod, it might have been able to deliver the same results, but I tend to doubt it. The est organization boasts that eventually all anyone will have to do to "get" the training is to send in their $250, but I doubt that would work either. The *presence* of the trainer is like an omnipresent mirror in which you are always asked to observe yourself. The trainer will always reflect back whatever image you put out there into the light with your own point of view and in such a way that you can see that your own point of view is a one-dimensional illusion.

Toward the end of the training, that solid, seemingly indestructible, all weather block of evaluations and judgments with which we usually identify ourselves begins to lose its critical mass and guess what happens when you look into the mirror?

There is nothing there.

("In the Japanese Shinto shrines there are no statues or effigies. They are empty except for a mirror in the center of the room to be used for "self-reflection.") "If you could really understand what it is to look into the empty mirror," said a Japanese Zen master to his student, "you would have no more work to do here."

"Today we're going to look at a thing we call reality," Ted said.

I yawned the moment that he said it. After all, what could he tell me about reality that I didn't already know? As the editor of the *East West Journal*, I had spent the last three years establishing a "consensus reality" that would allow us to take the next step in human cultural evolution; a reality based on the subtle, ever present energies of creation, and not the depleted fossil energies of the past. It seemed that the energies we lacked in our physical environment mirrored the lack of energy and consciousness we experience within our own lives.

And yet once that energy is found within, once the process of going unconscious is reversed, one opens himself up to energies that make all our attempts to harness energies in the past seem hopelessly obsolete.

I had already published an article by Christopher Bird, co-author of *The Secret Life of Plants*, in which he reported that Czechoslovakian scientists have built psychotronic generators that required only mental force to set them into perpetual motion. And there was the whole Uri Geller spoon-bending sideshow, and Thelma Moss's experiments with Kirlian photography and the human aura; there was acupuncture, and psychic surgery, and right on down the list. I didn't know where the energy originated that made these things possible, but I knew that it came from a source that didn't fit into any of our seventeenth-century, mechanistic notions about reality.

"The ultimate test for reality is physicalness," Rod said.

I was turned off immediately. I believed the ultimate test of reality to be nonphysical.

"That which is physical meets these agreements: It has form, distance, and time; it has energy or mass; and it exists in relationship to something else," he continued.

I was somewhat confused.

"What is the opposite of the blackboard?" he asked.

"No blackboard," someone replied.

It was beginning to sound like a high school lecture in the physical sciences. "Reality must be measurable," Rod said, as he began to set off a considerable measure of cynicism in me.

I knew that the reason science had not yet discovered, or been able to accept, the energies that were responsible for the phenomena mentioned previously was because they were difficult to measure in the laboratory.

Yankelovich writes about "measurability" in "The McNamara Fallacy":

> The first step is to measure what can easily be measured. This is O.K. as far as it goes. The second step is to disregard what can't be measured and give it an arbitrary . . . value. This is misleading. The third step is to presume that what can't be measured isn't very important. This is blindness. The fourth step is to say that what can't be measured doesn't really exist. This is suicide.

It should thus not come as a surprise to hear that scientists (men who believe in a measurable reality) have one of the highest occupational suicide rates in the world, or that Percy William Bridgeman, Nobel Prize 1946, wrote that he had still not unlocked the secrets of the physical universe prior to laying his head in an unlit gas oven, or that post-industrial, twentieth century civilization is presently choking in the charred dust of a dying planet Earth. A measurable reality.

"Reality is measurable," Rod said again.

It was as if I had stepped into an H. G. Wells time machine and been caught in the seventeenth century world of Descartes, Newton, and Kepler.

"And measurability is the ultimate test of physicalness."

I felt trapped in the room.

"I want you to take a look and see that how you know something is real is by how physical it is," he went on. "Thoughts are physical..."

They don't have mass, I thought, but according to all the work that has been done in biofeedback, they do have energy; and I had to admit that they also have form and distance in relation to something else.

"The way you know you love someone is physical. The way you feel when you feel happy is physical, and the way you know how you feel when you feel sad is physical." He was beginning to make sense, but there was something missing. "The ultimate test for reality is physicalness."

There was still something missing, and I resisted everything Rod said for the next hour. It was easy.

"And I'll tell you something else. Reality doesn't care about you."

It seemed true. Reality treats kings and pawns alike.

"I don't care about you," he chided, "anymore than gravity cares about you when it knocks you on your ass; it doesn't offer you any help either. Hey! Know what I do when someone asks me for help? I kick 'em right in the groin; help someone and he becomes helpless.

"Gravity is my guru.

"It tells me that if I jump off a building I'm going to hit the ground in pieces. So you know what?

"I don't go jumping off buildings.

"See, I know that most of you are still screwing around with gravity. That's why most of you look like you've been run over by buses. You think I'm kidding. Go take a look in the mirror."

It was growing increasingly uncomfortable in the room and the friendly, lighthearted atmosphere established earlier in the day seemed to evaporate each time Rod opened his mouth.

"You people think that we're all one, don't you? Well, I'll tell you something. I'm one, and you're still a bunch of assholes.

"I know what I'm saying isn't reasonable. Gravity isn't reasonable either. It ain't gonna be democratic in here. The universe is dictatorial.

"Too bad!"

What one experiences in the training is often out of context with what is being said or done, and sometimes, as I have mentioned, a series of psychological chain reactions may be set off. Rather than allow these things to rise to the surface, the mind will attempt to blot them out by going unconscious, as it does during boredom, tiredness, and sleep.

Brendan had mentioned during the first weekend that when people are asked in the processes to get in touch with certain parts of their bodies they will often go to sleep, as if on cue, whenever a part of the body is mentioned in which they are manifesting unconsciousness—the groin, for instance, or the heart. "All I've got to do is mention heart and a dozen people start to nod out," he said, "rather than experience the tightness, or sadness that is there."

At other times the will to "go unconscious" becomes so intense that the trainees will assault the trainer verbally. It is as if you are talking in your sleep and having a nightmare and someone comes along and wakes you up: You lash out at him before you are fully conscious of who and what he is.

Rod was going on, dealing with the trainees' questions about reality being physical. Since there is always a subtle transmission between gurus and their devotees, Rod's guru —gravity—was transmitting a certain physicalness, and implied aggression, through him. "Mess around with me and you'll wind up on your ass."

Steve, the potato of a man who had stood up on the first day of the training to ask Brendan to guarantee us that there would be no physical violence used in the training room, raised his hand to share.

Rod called on him about a half hour later.

"I'm really bored with what you are saying, and I don't

think you know what the hell you're talking about!" he said. His spudlike face turned beet-red with anger.

"Then why don't you leave?" Rod said, without raising his voice. "And if you think you can get someone else to tell you what you want to hear," he added coolly, but as if he were making a sincere suggestion, "go talk to him."

"I'm sure not going to hear it from you, buddy," Steve blurted, as the trainees went into a state of quiet tension.

"I'm sure you're not," Rod replied, still unflustered. "And we'll even give you your money back. How's that?"

Steve picked up his green school bag, threw his name tag on the floor, and stomped out of the room.

David Norris followed him out.

The trainees were wound up as tight as a clock with a mainspring that was about to snap. It seemed for a moment that they were going to break from their passivity, but then they sat back in their seats, attempting to unwind.

I watched Rod closely to see if he would exhibit any external signs of sentimentality, but he seemed as if he had already forgotten about what had occurred, and he casually moved into the next area of the discussion about reality.

"Anyone know why gravity doesn't need your say-so to knock you on your ass? . . . No one? . . .

"It's got an *agreement* going with the universe to do its things," he said, "and since it doesn't have a mind to put lots of 'I can't do it' considerations in the way, it always gets its job done, always!"

"What about people who can levitate?" someone asked.

"Good question," he said, "and I'd like to acknowledge you for asking it." It was the first time that he had done this. "People who can levitate have learned, have *experienced* how not to resist gravity, at least for a little while," he said. "But as far as the physical universe is concerned, what goes up must come down.

"That's the agreement. The universe works on agreement," he said, "and reality is a function of agreement and agreement alone."

I wondered how that related to physicalness. I also wondered what it meant.

"Things that have a lot of agreement on them are very massive," Rod said, pounding his fist against the wall. "And things that haven't got a lot of agreement on them, like all those considerations you have about not wanting to do what the boss tells you to do, are not very massive," he added.

"There's only one reason why your boss is boss." He began to tie it all in. "It's *agreement*. And if he doesn't get the job done, he gets his vote cancelled, losing his agreement the same way you do when you don't do what the boss tells you to do.

"Say, if you don't like having a boss, what you wanna get is that you set it up that way." He started to digress, but he returned to the subject with a simple dictum he would repeat every time someone asked a question.

"Reality is a function of agreement and agreement alone."

Simple or not, I wasn't sure what it meant.

"In order for something to be considered real, two or more people have to agree on it, and you know what the criteria for two people agreeing on something is besides its being physical? Anyone?" he asked. "Sandy? . . ."

"It's got to be reasonable enough or good enough for them to agree on," Sandy answered.

"Very good. It's got to be reasonable."

"Does that mean," a sophisticated woman in her late thirties began to ask, "that in order for something to be considered good, it's got to be reasonable as well as agreed-upon?"

"It does—and I know what you're driving at. You're going to tell me about all those paintings you have hidden in your basement that you think are so great," he said.

"I was," she said, as if surprised by Rod's quickness.

"Well, guess what? They're no good. They're not worth

anything except the salvage value of the materials they're painted on," he said.

The woman's cheeks burned.

"You know how you'll know if something is good or not?"

"By its artistic merit," the woman said.

"Bullllllllllshit, you do. The way to know how good something is is by its value. And you know how you know that? You know it by that little piece of paper on it called a price tag. Physicalness."

"What about those paintings that Van Gogh had hidden in his basement before they were sold, before anyone agreed they were good?" she asked. She was pulling at straws, and her breasts heaved as she sucked for air. She was very angry.

"Those paintings weren't any good. They were of no value. In order for something to have a value, it's gotta be out in the agreement," he said. "And you might want to take a look at your anger, and know that it's got nothing to do with what's going on between you and me."

The woman sat down.

"Thank you," Rod said.

                clapclapclapclapclapclap
                        clapclapclapclap
                              clap

She wasn't clear on it and neither was I.

"Reality is a function of agreement and agreement alone."

It began to dawn on me that Rod's constant repetition of this phrase was like a Zen koan.

        What is
                the sound
                        of one hand
                                clapping?

The solution to a koan* is usually so obvious that the student misses it as a result of all the effort he is putting into finding the answer.

Rod's constant repetition of "Reality is a function of agreement and agreement alone," did not take the form of a question, but he did say "If you could get this, your life would work."

I began to wonder whether I was missing the obvious, and chose to take the path of least resistance; to look and listen to what Rod was saying without trying to analyze or evaluate it.

As the editor of the *New Age Journal*, I had run an interview by Sam Keene with Carlos Castaneda, author of *A Separate Reality* and other books about his experiences with the sorcerer Don Juan. Sorcerers are not fond of statistics and the measurable reality of agreement, but Castaneda had said something in that interview that was very similar to what Rod was trying to put across.

> Don Juan says that there is much more to the world than we usually acknowledge. Our normal expectations about reality are determined by consensus [agreement]. We are taught how to see and understand the world. The trick of socialization is to convince us that the descriptions we agree upon define the limits of the real world.

I began to understand and accept what Rod was saying, even though I knew that what we call "reality" is only one way of seeing the world. I also began to see that only by "choosing the agreements," as we had been asked to do in the training, could one ever hope to gain enough votes to re-create the agreement to correspond with his reality.

There is only one way to change the agreement and that is to not try to change it but to take responsibility for it and

---

The dictionary defines *koan* as "a nonsense question to force a student, through contemplation of it, to a greater awareness of *reality*." Italics mine.

"make it your own." Actually, this is not as esoteric as it sounds, and there are many striking examples of it in the history of Western science. Although Copernicus knew by intuition that he had inherited a monster in the Ptolemaic theory that the earth was the center of a stationary universe, he did not set out by complaining or by trying to change the agreement. It was by working within the agreement, by totally accepting it as "what's so," by actually trying to strengthen the theory, that he was eventually able to establish its inconsistencies. It was his participation in the agreement, and not his resistance to it, that allowed him to gain enough evidence and votes to re-create the agreement to fit his reality.

Of course, this did not happen all at once. As George Leonard writes in *The Transformation*:

> It was like that in 1493 when men called Copernicus mad for saying the earth moved. But the earth did begin to move, and soon all humankind dwelled on a floating sphere that revolved in the heavens. And then the heavens themselves began to change. In the fifty years that followed Copernicus' proposal, Western astronomers first saw change in the previously immutable night sky. New stars appeared. Comets wandered at will through space that had been reserved for unchanging planets and stars.

In the training room, I recalled this passage about Copernicus and asked myself the obvious question: If one man's willingness to be responsible for the agreement could transform the entire universe, what effect would my willingness to be responsible for the agreement have on the Planet Earth?

But before I could begin to formulate a self-inspiring answer, I was distracted by a friend of mine, Rick, who got out of his seat in the third row and headed toward the back of the room.

He was about to push the swinging door open when David

Norris stopped him, sliding in between Rick and his aborted exit.

David stood with his back up against the door, and Rick, who was a head and a half taller and at least fifty muscular pounds heavier, huddled over him angrily.

I watched to see if David would show any signs of flinching, but he stood there steady as a rock.

It was a whispered exchange, but it sounded like two tomcats with their spines curled ready to put their lives on the line.

"I'm leaving the room!" Rick said.

"You're going right back to your seat and be responsible for your agreement," David snapped back in a snarled whisper.

Rick moved a few inches closer, and I thought he was going to pop him one any second.

David stared at him without blinking an eye.

"I'm going to the bathroom," Rick said, putting his hand on the door.

"You're going back to your seat," David replied, pushing his hand away. "You don't know—"

"I know I've got to go to the bathroom," Rick said, putting his hand back up on the door.

"You don't know the difference between your ass and a hole in the ground," David said, pushing his hand away again. "All the trainer has to do is talk about agreements, and you're ready to walk out of here and leave."

Rick took two steps to the right, pushed the door open, and walked out.

David followed him the same way he had followed Steve out earlier.

Rick was back in the room ten minutes later, and he raised his hand to share.

"Yeah, Rick," Rod said, "do you have a question?"

"I don't have a question," Rick replied, "and I'd like to share that I'm really, I mean literally, an asshole."

Rod laughed.

<pre>
       clapclapclapclapclapclapclap
              clapclapclap
                 clap
</pre>

"By the way, if something comes up like that again," Rod said, "I don't want to see any of you people tuning in. See, David keeps his job by keeping people in the room, so let him handle whoever has to be handled, and you keep looking up here."

"Who wants to look at you?" asked a trainee in the first row, looking to score points with his peers.

Rod was unmoved. "As far as I'm concerned, you can stare at the walls. There's one thing you people oughta get: It ain't no different in here than it is out there. Out there the ground rules are only implied. In here we make a point of being very clear on what they are. You keep the ground rules of this training, you choose them so that you're not the effect of them, and you'll be able to do the same thing on the outside.

"Keep the agreements and your life will work. Don't keep the agreements and your life won't work. It's as simple as that," he said. "Any questions?"

A short Puerto Rican fellow raised his hand.

"José?"

"What's the difference between being in here and being in prison?" José asked.

"No difference," Rod replied softly. "No difference, except for one: There are two kinds of prisons—maximum security prisons, with bars; and minimum security prisons, like here and on the outside, with doors."

Rod used this to illustrate that there are minority and majority agreements. "The bars work both ways, and the only thing that determines what side of the bars you're on is votes and the reasonableness of your behavior."

Very clever. I wondered if he had all his smart lines stored in vacuum-packed, airtight, corrosion-proof cans marked est, or if he made them up as he went along.

"That is to say," he went on, "that society is set up in such a way that if you break the rules enough times, you're going to have to deal with some pretty solid mass. Ask any of the people I trained at Lompoc Federal Penitentiary. They don't have any doubts about the fact that reality is physical.

"Know what happens when you try to resist that kind of reality? Anyone?"

"Attica," shouted a local hipster in the front row.

"Attica is a good example," Rod said. "See, institutions have an agreement going with gravity, and when you try to knock them over, they come tumbling down on top of you."

There were many other examples besides Attica. There was Kent State, and there was the National Guard, whose men, at the time the training was taking place, were still in the streets of Boston's South End. There was the march on Washington, the demonstrations at the Pentagon, and the rioting that took place in 1968 at the National Democratic Convention in Chicago. America had seen a movement that bore the pathetic title of the "resistance," a retreat from bayonet points and billy clubs in a hopeless attempt to try to "fix," "solve," "help," and "change things." Its one success had been to remove Lyndon Johnson from public office. And then what had happened? Richard Nixon, and an escalated war in Vietnam. "Resistance causes persistence." The problems had only changed form, and they continued to do so.

We are a nation at the level of effect.

If it wasn't the war in Vietnam, it was Watergate that was the cause of all our problems; and if it wasn't Richard Nixon, it was the Arabs; and if it wasn't the oil cartel, it was a failing economy; and if it wasn't inflation, it was New York City; and right on down to the stalled assembly lines of GM's Vega plant in Lordstown, Ohio. Strike!

Anything so as not to take responsibility for our lives not working.

"What is" between us as individuals and "being with

other people" created the Pentagon, My Lai, and racial rioting in the streets of Boston. "What is" between us and the things we repress rather than experience in our lives created Attica, Kent State, and all those repressive institutions that we call collectively the "military-industrial complex."

How could that have anything to do with me? I asked myself.

"If you're not responsible for your experience, who is? Who is?" Rod asked in reference to a woman's question.

She was unwilling to accept that she was responsible for the murder of six million Jews, or the starvation of a million Biafran children, or the thousands who had lost their lives in the Chilean earthquake.

And so was I.

"It's a difficult thing for the linear mind to get," Rod said. "We'll deal with it again tomorrow," he concluded, leaving us hanging with the burden of guilt.

Rod continued to talk about reality.

"What's the opposite of reality?" asked Frances, a woman in her late fifties who wore a large tortoise-shell barrette in her hair.

"What's the opposite of the blackboard?" Rod replied.

"No blackboard," Frances said.

"And how do you know there's no blackboard?"

It was so obvious that Frances was stumped by the question.

"Someone else?" Rod asked.

"I can't see it," said Bill, a pharmaceutical salesman.

"And what else can't you do with it?" Rod asked.

"I can't measure it. I can't touch it. It has no mass and it doesn't exist in time." Bill was beginning to catch on. "It's an illusion."

"That's right," Rod said, "The opposite of reality is the experience of the illusion. And what happens when we look at our experience and tell the truth about it? It disapppears!

"I want you to take a look at the thing we call time. It

isn't physical. It has no mass or energy, and it isn't solid. Time is an illusion, and everything that we have been talking about as reality exists in time and only with respect to our point of view.

"That is to say, before the blackboard was a blackboard, it was wood, metal, and whatever else it is made of, and if you begin to look at it outside of time—what happens?"

"It disappears," Bill said.

"So guess what?" Rod asked, in such a way that I knew he was leading up to something big. "What we've been calling reality is really an illusion."

The trainees burst into laughter, and so did Rod.

No wonder I had felt incomplete about what Rod was saying earlier. But if he had begun by saying that reality is an illusion, I would never have been able to "get" that the universe works on agreement. Nor would I have been able to know that in order to make my life work, I had to be willing to take responsibility for whatever the agreements were.

I began to feel a sense of exhilaration, along with a total willingness to be in the room.

At that point Rod called a bathroom break.

During the break I saw Steve, the man who had left the room, and, I thought, the training, in disgust. I was surprised he was still hanging around.

He was chatting with at least a half dozen people, lapping up the approval he was receiving for his "courageous" action.

"I thought you left," I said.

"I never left. David talked to me. And I told him that I had had a hard night and that I was gonzo, and I was back in the room ten minutes later."

"Back to your seats," hollered one of the assistants. "We're about to begin.

As I made the door, I was still fiddling with my name tag.

I was stopped by Ivan.

"You can't come in the room until your name tag is on," he said.

It was half on already, but I stepped aside. "Well, if that's the agreement—"

Rod was already warmed up and ready to begin. "The things that exist in what we call reality only exist with respect to our point of view, and that is established by consensus."

Castaneda said that he came to understand reality in terms of Talcott Parsons's idea of "glosses":

> A gloss is a total system of perception and language. . . . This room is a gloss. We have lumped together a series of isolated perceptions—floor, ceiling, window, lights, rugs, etc., to make a single totality. A child reconnoiters the world with few preconceptions until he is taught to see things in a way that everybody agrees upon. The world is an agreement.

"What artists do," Rod said, "is to rearrange the descriptions from time to time."

Vincent van Gogh, for example, rearranged our descriptions of the heavens when he painted "Starry Night." Instead of portraying the stars as dead hunks of matter moving in the black void of space, he painted them in a new way: Stars are alive and they whirl around in an energy field of an expanding universe.

Still that is only rearranging the descriptions. It is only a different interpretation. What Erhard has done in the est training has been to create a space in which people slip between descriptions and see that no description is final. When that happens, you stop the world and see. As Don Juan says, "you are left with wonder, the true wonder of seeing the world without interpretation."

Several months after I had completed the training, I heard one teenager describe what happened to him after he took the "teen training." "I walked out into a field and saw a hole in the ground. I said 'Look! That's . . . a hole! Look at it! Look at it! That's a . . . hole. And look over here! Look. That's a tree. That's a . . . rock.' I was able to see it without adding or subtracting anything."

Although it is said that seeing is believing, to see without believing is to look and wonder, to really see.

"The problem with most people is that they are stuck in their point of view," Rod said.

I knew that I had spent a good part of my life stuck in mine. Not seeing.

"And when you get off your point of view—all that you're left with is your experience," he added excitedly.

"Anyone know where you experience your experience?" he asked.

"In my aching back," said Charlie.

"Want me to make your aching back go away?"

"Are you serious?"

"I'm serious. All I've got to do is cut off one of your fingers and you'll find you don't experience your experiences in your back."

"I experience it in my head, then," the person said.

"Oh, yeah? Then why does your back hurt?"

He started to say something, but Rod interrupted him.

"You people don't know where you experience your experience, do you?" he asked. "All you can do is notice what you are experiencing. And when you look at your experience, and accept responsibility for being the source of it—what happens?"

"It disappears," said Charlie, adding that his back was longer aching.

"So when you experience the truth, you know it's nothing but an illusion!" Rod said, orchestrating the symphony into its final movement.

"Then how did all this stuff get here?" someone asked.

"It never did," Rod said.

I was beginning to feel myself moving into a state of

consciousness that I had previously experienced only in meditation. It was accompanied by the physical sensation that someone was lifting an enormous rock off the top of my head.

Rod was looking more and more like a Zen master, and I wondered if he had been one in another lifetime. At any rate, he was looking less and less like the high-school science teacher with whom I had previously compared him.

"Then what caused it?" another person asked.

"There is no cause in the illusion—it's all effect! It's like the domino theory.

"OK, let's take an example—house. What caused the house? House is a concept made out of a construct—wood. Did the wood cause the house? No. Wood is a concept made out of a construct—water and fiber. Did the water and fiber cause the house? Did it cause the wood? No. Water and fiber are concepts made out of constructs—hydrogen, oxygen and carbon. Did these cause the house? Did they cause the water and fiber? No. Hydrogen, oxygen, and carbon are concepts made out of constructs—electrons, protons, and neutrons. Did these cause the house, or the hydrogen, or the water and fiber, or the wood? No. Electrons and protons are concepts made out of— All the way the way back to infinity.

"The closest we can get to what caused the house is that it is an effect of your point of view, in time.

"In the illusion that we call reality, there's no cause. It's effect! Effect! Effect!

"Well, who created the universe?" Charlie asked.

"In your universe you're God," Rod said, "you caused it, and pretended not to cause it so you could play in it.

"And there are at least as many the universes as there are people on this planet.

"It all comes out of your point of view."

"Well, what created my point of view?" Charlie asked, like a seasoned philosopher.

"You did," Rod said. He started to say something else,

but stopped. "We'll talk more about the source of that movement tomorrow."

I thought of a Zen story I had once read.

A couple of students were walking through a village with their master and came across a flagpole.

"Is it the flag that's moving or the flagpole?" asked the Zen master.

"It's the flag," answered one student.

"It's the flagpole," answered the other.

"It is neither," answered the master. "The movement is in your own mind."

Chapter VI

SUCCESSIVE MOMENTS OF NOW

I went into the fourth day of the training zapped up in a sleepless state of semi-euphoria, with the attitude that I had already "gotten" whatever there was to "get." I had ridden high on the est roller coaster the previous day. I was thus caught unaware and felt my stomach dropping as the cart plunged deeply into the final turn.

Rod Logan began the session by telling us "The end is the beginning," and "I ain't told you turkeys nothin' yet." It was the first time that he hadn't referred to us as a bunch of assholes. "Now that you know that which direction is up depends on your point of view, you also know the difference between your ass and a hole in the ground," he said. "So congratulations. I'll now refer to you as turkeys."

It was a backhanded compliment.

"Turkeys are so stupid that when it rains outside, they leave the roost to go out to take a drink of water," he said, opening his mouth and looking at the ceiling, "and they drown because they forget to close their mouths. Turkeys are so stupid—" He went on with at least a half dozen insulting comparisons.

A rotund fellow in the center section, with a scraggly beard that made him look like a cross between Rutherford

B. Hayes and Millard Fillmore, raised his hand in the middle of the last turkey joke.

"Peter? Question about being a turkey?" Rod asked.

"I don't know whether I should say this or not," Peter said, "but the person sitting next to me is eating Life Savers."

"I'd like you to get, Peter, that Life Savers aren't going to save his ass. Whether you should say it or not depends upon whether you expect to win approval for saying it," Rod said. "Anyway, I'm glad you did. Will someone on the logistics team pick up those Life Savers?" Rod asked, addressing David Norris.

"You people will do anything to get approval. Anything! You'll go through life getting all beat up—you'll even die —if it means you're going to get someone else's approval. There's only one thing you want more than approval, and that's to be right. Did Brendan tell you the story about the rat and the cheese?" he asked.

He had, but no one said anything and Rod launched into his own comical version of it anyway.

"Virtually everything we know about human behavior, we know from experiments conducted with white rats and college sophomores, neither of which may be human. I don't know much about college sophomores, but I can speak with some authority about white rats. You see, if you take a white rat and put him in front of a series of tunnels, and put cheese down the third tunnel, eventually the rat will come up with the cheese. Rats don't care if you like them. They don't care who said what. They ain't interested in good ideas. Rats only know from cheese. They're interested in cheese. And if you put the cheese in the third tunnel, every time you put the rat in the maze he'll go right down the third tunnel and get the cheese. Now, if you take the cheese out, the rat will still go straight down the third tunnel. No cheese. Come back out, look around. Go back down the third tunnel. Look around. No cheese. Back out. Look around. Back down the third tunnel. No cheese. The difference between a white rat and a human being is that eventually the white rat will give up the third tunnel, and a human being will keep on going down it forever." (Laughter.)

            clapclapclapclapclap
                      clapclapclapclapclapclap
                                clapclapclapclap

"Thank you...

"You see, human beings ain't much interested in cheese. Human beings are very much into 'right.' I know that's a terrible thing to tell you. I mean, after all, I know you're interested in being nurtured and loving, self-expressive and healthy. Yeah? Yeah? I'll bet you'd rather be right. I'd bet you'd rather be right.

"You've spent your whole lives being right! And where has it gotten you? Right here! Right here! And being where you're at in your life makes you so uncomfortable that you're willing to pay some asshole two hundred and fifty dollars to stand up and call you a turkey.

"See? Being right doesn't work. And once you begin to 'get' that—and you all have or you wouldn't be here—you'll try something else. And when that doesn't work, you'll try something else. And when that doesn't work, you'll try something else, until you begin to 'get' . . . that nothing works!" Rod shouted.

My euphoria began to vanish, as it had the morning Rod walked into the training room.

"Do you think it's going to get any better after you walk out of here tonight?" Rod asked. "Well, get ready for a big surprise. I want to tell you that the same old stuff is going to come up, and that it may upset you as much as it ever did before. But the chances are that you're going to be able to handle it in such a way that you're no longer the effect of it—unless you are, unless you are. . . .

"Have you ever tried to get better? Have you ever tried to change something about yourself that you didn't like?"

Lao-tsu said, "Don't struggle," but I saw the direction that Rod was heading, and I was struggling not to accept it.

Had I endured this much of the training only to be told that absolutely nothing works?

"It's all going to be the same?" someone asked.

"It is if you say it is," Rod said. "It is if you *try* to make it any better."

We had been told by Brendan that all the effort we were putting into making our lives work was keeping us "below the line." And on the other side of that line was "acceptance, aliveness, and expanding satisfaction in life."

"The one thing that is keeping you people 'in effort,' the one thing that makes it all such a struggle, is your mind.

"So today we're going to take a look at the mind. We're going to see how it's wired up and what its design function is. And by this evening, your mind is going to stop. It's going to die."

The person sitting next to me was sweating it out.

Rod went on, "By the end of the training today, you're going to see what it's like to live without any of the considerations that the mind usually puts in the way. Not as a concept or an intellectual exercise but as an experience."

I was sure that there were people in the room who thought he was talking about a prefrontal lobotomy.

"Did Brendan tell you that you were all going to 'get it' before the end of the training? Well, you are. You're all going to have a chance to go 'Aha! Aha, this is it!' "

Rod was winding himself up.

"See, people have this incredible notion that they *are* their minds.

"Well, it's a lie," he said.

It was thus that Rod began an incredible discussion of the human mind. It was to last more than eleven hours, during which time I realized that it didn't have to be dark outside for me to go to sleep.

"What is the mind's principal function?" asked Rod.

Hands were raised all around the room.

"Everyone is going to get a chance to share his opinion on this one," said Rod. He asked everyone in the room to stand.

One by one, starting with the left side of the room, opinions started flying in every conceivable direction.

"The mind is a trap," said a woman in the first row.

"It's a little voice that tells you you can never be satisfied with what you don't really want," said the man sitting next to her, hoping to hit the nail right on the head, for the mind is "into" being right.

One by one, the trainees sat down, and then proceeded to think about what they should have said or would say given another opportunity.

"The mind is the seat of all intelligence, the source of progress, and our only hope for the future of mankind," said a gentleman with thick gray hair who was not only a professor at MIT, but also a former member of Herman Kahn's "Commission on the Year 2000."

"The mind is an ocean of infinite possibilities."

"Ego."

"A living hell."

"Our link to heaven."

"A closed door."

"A wild monkey."

"A chatterbox."

"A sword that cuts through all the bullshit."

"An assembly line that puts together all that we know and all that we don't know, and comes up with a belief system called truth."

"A silver locket filled with human excrement."

"A mirror."

"A Chinese box."

And on . . .
        and on . . .
               and on . . .
until everybody in the room was sitting again.

"You're all wrong!" exclaimed Rod. "The mind's principal function is survival. The mind will do anything to survive. Anything . . . anything!" Rod looked leerily around the room. "If you think I'm kidding, take a look at those times in your life when your survival has been threatened. Take a look. What your mind did was resist . . .

"I'm not saying it's bad to resist. In some circumstances, it may be appropriate. I'm saying that when almost every situation you have to deal with starts to constitute a threat to your survival, you have to pay a very high price for your resistance. It costs you your 'aliveness,' your health, your happiness— More on that later.

"Right now all I want you to 'get' is that the mind resists any situation that makes you uncomfortable."

It was hot and stuffy in the room and the psychological pressure began to mount; I squirmed in my seat, but there was no escape from the smothering atmosphere.

Most of the trainees had gone into the last day of the training thinking, as I did, that the worst of it was over; but the worst was yet to come. And all the boredom, anger, fear, anxiety, and contempt for the trainer that we had experienced on the earlier days of the training was being reactivated unconsciously. It came back like a returning infection, and it was resisted like one.

"If you think that a little ole bacteria climbed into bed with you and caused you to come down with the flu, you're crazy. You got sick because the mind wanted you to get sick, and maybe because it wanted somebody else's approval," Rod said.

"You know what we do around the est office in San Francisco when people complain about being sick? We shove em off the third-floor fire escape. That's what we do. You either come in to work or you have the doctor call us and tell us you're laid up in the hospital."

I was tired of hearing Rod's rap; the time began to pass so slowly that sometimes a second in Rod's universe of personal responsibility seemed like an eternity in hell.

"What you want to 'get,'" he went on, "is that when you can be with the things in your life that make you uncomfortable, your life expands," Rod said. "When you stop resisting all those things you've been struggling with"—he took out a handkerchief and blew his nose—"they begin to dissolve.

"But you don't believe that, do you?" he asked sarcastically. "So in a minute we're going to give you a chance to share your considerations."

Rod took a sip of tea from an insulated metal container that was kept filled by the training supervisor throughout the training. David Norris would deliver it to him periodically, walking quietly up to the platform like a vassal of the prelate bringing holy water to a pope.

"It's funny," Rod said. "I'm sitting up here drinking tea, and you're the ones who have to go to the bathroom." He waved the container in front of the trainees as mercilessly as an emperor pointing thumbs down to indicate the fate of two hundred and fifty Christians in the arena.

"It all comes out of survival, people," he said smacking his lips. "It all comes out of survival," he repeated, opening the floor to the trainees' unending considerations.

They were throwing themselves against a lion, and he ingested them one by one.

I had already "gotten" what Rod was saying about survival and I grew excruciatingly bored as hand after hand raised consideration after consideration, only to be ripped open by the thrust of the lion's claw.

"Couldn't we move on to something more interesting?" a trainee asked.

"We'll move on after everyone who has any considerations gets a chance to share them; and I want you to get that wanting things to be interesting is your act. It is the way your mind has picked out for you to avoid the things you don't want to handle," he said. "It is your way of going unconscious, and you probably can't be with people unless they're interesting."

He was hitting the nail right on my head.

Though it was only on rare occasions that Rod let people get too far before he pounced on them, I began to notice his effervescent willingness to stick it out with them until they 'got' what he was saying. I had only to listen to people's considerations; he had to wrestle with them fifteen hours straight, on two consecutive days, every weekend. The energy that he was willing to put into the match seldom varied, whether it was nine A.M. or three o'clock in the morning.

It was the same with Brendan, and it is the same with all the other est trainers, including Werner Erhard. Brendan had said that Werner and the other trainers once spent thirteen hours dealing with a single consideration he had about wanting to go to the mountains.

"You people are going to be here all night," Rod shouted. Every time he wrote a piece of data on one of the blackboards, some smart turkey would raise his hand to present the one exception to the rule.

"I want to share with you how to do this training successfully," Rod said. "All you have to do is 'get' where I'm coming from. I'm not asking you to agree with me. And I'm not asking you to refrain from sharing your considerations, whatever they are. But 'get' where I'm coming from. The things I'm sharing with you are not rules. Werner says, 'There are no rules except one, and that is that there are no rules.'

"So don't waste your time and mine trying to break rules that don't exist. Also, don't waste your time trying to make a rule out of anything I've said, because you'll find the one exception to that rule in your life, and it won't work.

"What Werner has done is to create a model so close to the way things actually are that when you lay it over the things you've been stuck on, those things become transparent. I mean they dissolve and disappear—kaput!

"Now, I've known a lot of brilliant guys in my life, who have said some very bright things"—Rod used to be involved in politics and the law—"none of which I've ever been able to apply. And then I met Werner and started hanging out with him, and I would take what he said and use it in my speeches, or in court, and it would work every time. I began to notice that whatever I picked up from Werner worked.

"The guy's a genius. I mean it," Rod said, "and all I am doing is re-creating for you the things Werner has said to me that have worked in my life. Everybody clear on that now?"

I was touched by Rod's tribute to Werner. I thought Rod to be the only person in the room with an ego as enormous as mine, and yet every time he mentioned Werner's name, it was with utter deference and respect. It wasn't the kind I had seen thrown at the feet of Sri Whatsisnami or gilded gurus in saffron robes. It was the kind of practical respect one would have for a Rolls-Royce or a Mercedes-Benz. I knew Rod had bought Werner's rap because it was the finest vehicle that he had found on the road to his own enlightenment.

"The mind is a linearly arranged, multi-sensory, total record of successive moments of now," Rod said. "Code name *stack*."

Rod began to write down some new data on the anatomy of the mind. "By the way, the linear mind can't understand this, so don't try to figure it out," he added, repeating that "the mind is a linearly arranged, multi-sensory, total record of successive moments of now . . . code name *stack*."

Rod explained that the "records" are the sum total of the human experience, including three and one-half billion years of biological development, and another three hundred and fifty billion years of creation. It is because of the linear arrangement of the mind (using the body and its physical location as its point of view) that the potential range of human consciousness is usually sacrificed to the isolated perception of scattered events in time.

"What you recall experiencing," Rod said, "comes out of

your point of view, and the rest is unexperienced experience."

It is easy to see why Ptolemy thought the earth to be the center of a stationary universe whose creation took place as an isolated event in time. Using his body and its physical location as his point of view, it was. It is not so easy to see why mystics long before the second century A.D., when Ptolemy advanced his view, thought the earth to be a whirling mass of energy moving along with the rest of the universe at a speed of infinite expansion. The source of this information, according to mystical tradition, was something called the *Akashic Records* (code name *stack*), a psychic storehouse of data on everything that ever happened on this planet or in the universe itself. One had only to project his consciousness into the *Akashic*, it is said, in order to find out what he wanted to know, on instant replay.

In that process, linear time would vanish into "successive moments of now," and the body was lost or "dropped" as a point of view. (The mind resists this expansion of consciousness; since the body is its point of view, it resists its "loss" as a threat to survival.)

Although this sort of thing is referred to in the training as "mystical bullshit," it does not contradict anything that is said in est. In fact, it tends to affirm what actually is said at the end of several processes, namely, "I am powerful and have the power to project my consciousness anywhere in the universe, providing it is ethical."

"The mind is a linearly arranged, multi-sensory, total record," Rod kept reminding us, "of successive moments of now . . . code name *stack*. And begin to 'get' that the mind will use anything that you are unwilling to experience as a threat to survival. I.e., vital shock.

"What you are unwilling to experience runs you," Rod said. "The whole universe is running you, and you can't even see it because your minds are keeping you stuck in your point of view.

"The mind is a linearly arranged, multi-sensory, total

record of successive moments of now . . . code name *stack*. Don't try to figure it out."

At this point in the training I began to notice that there wasn't any problem in my life that I couldn't make disappear by stepping outside my point of view. I also began to notice that the only reason I could have noticed this in the first place was that I was actually beginning to step out of my linear mind.

Almost every spiritual discipline that has ever existed on the face of this planet (including organized religion) has had as its traditional aim the disappearance of the linear mind (although it may not have been called that). To lose oneself in God is to lose one's linear mind, and the experience is often referred to as "divine madness"; the beatified person is "crazy drunk on God." Some of the techniques that have been developed for this are bhakti devotional chanting, meditation, and prayer, zikr (the whirling dance of dervish ecstasy), the repetition of a sacred word or mantra ("Om mani padme hum, Om . . ."), and even contemplation as practiced by Newton and by a twelfth-century Irish monk who wrote a book called *The Cloud of the Unknowing*. I want to be clear that all of these practices work.

And that they haven't worked.

If they had worked for enough people, our planet would not be in the state of crisis it is now in as a result of our linear, survival-bound orientation. The lines on the map of the earth represent our linear point of view in time, and even though our astronauts tell us they are actually imaginary, a half-million people chanting "Hari Krishna" to the grace of God have not been able to make them disappear.

What Erhard has done has been to develop a training that is synchromesh with the electrified pace of the twentieth-century, post-industrial culture—a training in which one can lose his linear mind in two weekends in places like New York, Chicago, Los Angeles, and Boston—and all within the unglamorous context of a hotel room. It is not a technique in the traditional sense of the word; the training produces the results at which other techniques are aimed, and it does not end until those results are produced.

"Getting the job done," Erhard calls it; and "getting the job done"—for Erhard—also implies training enough people to change the "critical mass" of the physical universe into an enlightened humanity. Whether he will be able to produce the results remains to be seen, but it is interesting to note that a traditional Zen master was lucky to train ten followers in his lifetime, one of whom had the potential to carry on the lineage. Erhard has trained over sixty-five thousand people in three short years, nine of whom can deliver the training as effectively as he can. Enlightenment is a greasy question when you look at it in terms of statistics, but Erhard is only thirty-eight years old, and one cannot deny him the exponential possibility of getting the job done and getting the physical universe to work.

Back in the training room, Rod began to wrap it up, constantly repeating that "The mind is a linearly arranged, multi-sensory, total record of successive moments of now ... code name *stack*."

I was beginning to "get it." I experienced my mind moving from one topic to the next without pausing to reflect on its own occasional brilliance. It was as if my mind were a fluorescent light, flickering on and off so fast that when it was off, it truly seemed to be on. I watched the room grow very bright, as if someone had brought in the sun in a donkey cart; and I was able to penetrate the deepest questions that emerged in the successive reappearance of my linear mind.

And then I started to "get" that this wasn't "it" at all. It was not in the steady stream of realizations that seemed to be flowing from the wellspring of my linear mind. It was in the momentary absence of this flood that I felt a certain transformation taking place.

Buddha once said, "There are three trillion thoughts that

pass through the mind in the time it takes to blink one's eye." (Talk about "informational anxiety"—for the mind, it is a chronic state.) Buddha also said that to be without thoughts for twelve seconds is to launch oneself into samadhi, enlightenment.

I knew that what I was experiencing was not the samadhi that Buddha was talking about; thoughts seemed to flow from my mind at an accelerating rate of mental speed, and yet I cannot deny that there were moments, if not seconds, when it all seemed to stop.

Though these moments exist without description, perhaps this Zen waka poem by Miyamoto Musashi, a sixteenth-century samurai, will convey a sense of what they were like.

> Into a mind that is absolutely free from
>   thoughts and emotions,
> Even the tiger finds no room to insert
>   its fierce claws . . .
>
> No thinking, no reflecting—
>   perfect emptiness
> Yet therein something moves,
>   following its own course.
>
> The eye sees it,
>   but no hand can take hold of it—
> The moon in the stream:
>   this is the secret of my school.

The silent mind, the moon in the stream. It was worth all the boredom, all the anger, all the tears, all the joy—it was worth all of it; and even though this collection of moments could have lasted no more than a few seconds, I knew that in them I experienced eternity.

"The mind is a linearly arranged, multi-sensory, total record of successive moments of now," Rod snapped.

The woman who had argued with Rod about art and

aesthetics stood up in tears. "I feel as if I am going to faint. . . . My mind is disappearing and I don't want to let go of it," she said.

"Stay with your experience," Rod said unsentimentally, "and"—softening his voice—"you can choose not to faint." He went on: "One other thing—The resistance you are experiencing is your mind fighting for its survival. Acknowledge your mind for doing its job, and know that at this point it will do anything to make you go unconscious."

The woman smiled and regained her composure.

clapclapclapclapclapclapclapclapclapclap
        clapclapclapclapclapclapclapclap
               clap

"I feel as if I'm being brainwashed," a trainee shared.

"I want you to notice that brainwashing is a concept that your mind is wrapping around your experience of having no mind," Rod said.

We were being brainwashed "Tide-clean," but not in the traditional way, where one belief system is merely exchanged for another. There was nothing being put back in, nothing.

It was at this point in the training that, as one graduate reported to a journalist, "They could have told me anything." At a later point in the evening, Rod told us that the building was on fire, and that they had arranged for a dozen elephants to take us to another hotel.

I fell for it hook, line, and sinker, wondering how they had made the arrangements so quickly.

"The mind is a linearly arranged, multi-sensory, total record of successive moments of now," Rod said, asking us to repeat it with him.

After repeating this aloud along with the 250 other trainees, I began to wonder whether the phrase might not also be something like a Zen koan.

"What is the sound of one hand clapping?"
(One has only to listen to the silence.)

But then again, a koan usually takes the form of a question. This was clearly not a question, and it required no solution. It was not long, however, before I began to link it up with a couple of things Rod had said earlier in the evening. "What Werner has done is to create a model so close to the way things actually are that when you lay it over the things you've been stuck on, they become transparent and disappear."

I also recalled an exercise in which we were told to bring two imaginary pieces of chalk into the same space. In the moment when we brought them together, there truly seemed to be nothing there.

"The mind is a linearly arranged, multi-sensory—" Erhard's model of the mind is so close to the way the mind actually is that when you bring the two into the same space they both disappear, if only for the blink of an eye. Long enough to experience the absence of three trillion thoughts in your head.

And even if it hadn't disappeared for a full thirteen seconds, I now began to know that the whole training was about disappearance. On the first day of the training we had disappeared "how we know we know by looking through our eyes with our eyes—seeing what we see from where we see it." On the second day we disappeared our items (our unexperienced experience) by re-creating them in the truth process. On the third day of the training, we disappeared reality, with a model that was now so obvious that my original resistance to it seemed absurd. "Reality is a function of agreement, and agreement alone." On the fourth day, we were disappearing our minds as the source of the illusion.

"Getting it" ordinarily means to add something to what you have, but it seemed that what we were "getting" was nothing.

"What do you have to know in order for you to know you 'got' the training?" Rod asked.

"Nothingggggggggg," we replied in unison, some with sighs of relief, others in bitter disappointment.

"What has to happen in order for you to experience that you 'got' the training?" Rod was beginning to lighten up.

"Nothingggggggggggg," we replied again.

Hadn't trainer Randy McNamara said, "The training is about nothing; and it ain't nothing like you've ever seen"?

"All right," Rod said. "At this point you either know you 'got' the training, or you know you didn't 'get' the training, or you're not sure whether you 'got it' or not."

He asked those of us who knew they hadn't "gotten it" or weren't sure, to stand. And then one by one he began to handle everyone's consideration about whether he had "gotten it" or not. Rod circled the room like a hawk, hovering over those who were resisting "getting" that they "got it." "What is, is, and what ain't, ain't. Get it?"

The people who weren't sure whether they had "gotten it" began to sit down, and the people who *knew* they hadn't "gotten it" moved up to not being sure. After an hour or so, there was only one person left standing, John Demartino.

He was big and husky and looked more as if he were about to graduate from a New England tractor-trailer school than from the est training. He was standing near the aisle on the left side of the room. I remembered him because during the second day he had "shared" that his item was anger, and this went well with my picture of him.

Rod was standing about twenty feet away from him, on the other side of the center aisle.

"I felt anger when you were over there," John said.

Rod saw something in John's face that was clearly invisible to me. He raced down the center aisle toward the platform and then back up the right aisle toward John. "OK, John, what is it?"

John tried to hold back, but he broke down, crying.

"Describe your experience. What do you see?" Rod

asked standing about two inches away from John's face. "I'll take care of that," he said, taking the microphone. "What do you see?"

"My grandfahthah's funeral." John had a Boston accent.

"Stay with your experience. Go on, John. Go on. What's going on at your grandfather's funeral?"

"The grown-ups and the relatives are standing around, and they're all so fucking stern, and they're all so fucking serious. I feel very angry and—I want to—" John broke off and started bawling again.

"What do you want to do, John? Stay with your experience, and tell me what you want to do," Rod cajoled. "Come on, John, what do you wanna do?"

"I want to walk over to the casket and tell him that I love him," he said, no longer making any effort to hold back the tears.

"OK, John, OK. Walk over to the casket and tell your grandfather that you love him," Rod said.

Throughout this dialogue, John had stood with his eyes cast toward the floor, but he suddenly looked up into the "safe space" of the training room and said, "I love you, gramps . . . I love you."

It was the first point in the training that I actually felt tears come to my eyes.

clapclapclapclapclapclap
clapclapclapclapclapclap
clapclap

Rod walked back to the platform. "Very nice, John, very nice . . . Now, that may come up again, and it may not. If it does, look at it and describe your experience."

"One other thing I might mention to all of you, if you're still holding onto something after you walk out of here tonight: I can guarantee that it is going to run you like a machine.

"But will that mean you didn't 'get' the training? No. It'll just mean that you still have stuff to deal with like the rest of us."

It was the first time that he included himself as a member of the group, and as he said it he walked off the platform in the front of the room.

"If you walk out of here tonight and things don't appear to be any better . . . if all your problems aren't solved . . . will that mean you didn't get the training?"

"Noooooooooooooooooooooooooooooooooooo."

We had been looking into the mirror for over fifty hours. We had seen the best and worst of ourselves, and nary a one was empty.

"All you can do is accept what's there," Rod said. "Take what you get."

The last time I had heard that phrase, it had been in the agreements. "Keep your ass in the room; your soles on the floor. Follow the instructions and take what you get."

It had never occurred to me until now that to "take what you get" could have meant to "accept what is." Nor had it occurred to me that simply by following the instructions, the ground rules of the training, I would be able to accept —as far as my life was concerned—that "what is, is, and what ain't, ain't." I had always thought of "taking it" in terms of getting "beat up," but the one thing that was beating me was my resistance to my problems.

I had once seen a demonstration by an Aikido master who instructed one of his students to take hold of his wrist. The student did so, and the master tried to resist his grip. "Do you see what happens when I resist?" The more he tried to pull away, the more of his body he lost to the student's control. "Now see what happens when I let go . . ." He relaxed his whole body around his wrist. "I now can move in any direction I choose." At that point he flattened the student on the bamboo mat.

"I'll tell you how to flatten your problems." Rod said, "Give them space. If someone throws a punch at you"—

he had turned right into my metaphor—"give it enough space, and it won't become a problem.

"Unless it does. Unless it does.

"You know what life would be like without any problems? Let me tell you.

"Werner has a training that he doesn't talk about too much. And it works very simply. We take you to a surgeon, and he cuts out all your organs, and then we bathe your body in tepid water for the next three years.

"That's what life would be like without any problems."

I began to see that he was leading us into the realization that this is a perfectly imperfect universe, and I still wondered if this indeed were the best of all possible worlds.

"When you begin to take responsibility for your life, you also begin to take responsibility for the world; but if you take responsibility for your life, the world will take care of itself.

"Let guys like me and Werner worry about the world.

"See, we love our problems, but we don't get stuck solving the same old problems over and over again. We look for new ones, and that's why Werner created the game called est. And he sits back there in San Francisco, doing whatever it is that he does, creating problems for other people to solve. That's what's called being the source of the game."

I sat in my seat asking myself that if life was always going to be filled with problems, no matter how good at solving those problems I got, how could I ever expect it to work? It wasn't until three months later, when I attended a special graduate event in New York City entitled "Something about Nothing," that I discovered the answer.

I sat in my seat asking myself how I could ever expect life to work; and it was with Rod's parting words that I discovered the answer.

"Life doesn't work," he said, "it never has, and it never will—I know that may be hard to get, but no matter what you do, it won't work, and no matter what you think it won't work, and no matter who you become—it's never going to work.

"But you know what . . . It doesn't even mean anything that life doesn't work. It isn't even bad that life doesn't work. So here's a suggestion, and it's one of the most valuable ones I've picked up from Werner.

"Stop trying to make life work. When you stop trying to make life work you won't have to struggle anymore; you will have nothing to do; you will have literally nothing to do.

"And that creates the space for you to discover that you are; that's the only thing there is to get."

The trainees left Conference Room A that evening wrapped in a blanket of euphoria. They didn't know how or why, and they didn't care. They had nothing. They expected nothing. And they knew they had already "gotten" whatever it was they needed to get. It was a realization that they would be able to apply in the coming months as they began to expand their own ground of being.

I left Howard Johnson's that night tasting a mixture of twenty-seven flavors of emotion. I had spent more than the allotted sixty hours with the people in the training room, and I didn't want to see them disappear into graduation night forever. "And the space, man, the space!" I heard one graduate exclaim as we left the "safe space" of the est training room. There would be other opportunities to plug into it, and in the coming weeks I would look forward to them.

Night danced into morning as I hit the expressway. It would soon be rush hour, and I could already hear the truck horns.

The world was exactly the same, and totally different.

Chapter VII

THE MASTERY OF LIFE

The Statler Hilton was once considered one of Boston's grand hotels, but its elegant lobby now looks like a cross between the Great Hall of the People and a littered penny arcade. On sale in the vestibule is the worst in imitation art, and the best in airlines: Pan Am, TWA, Swissair, Sabena, and BOAC. Perhaps the only redeeming quality of the hotel is Trader Vic's, where I am sitting next to a stranger whose varicose veins outline the huge black bags beneath his eyes.

He looks like Robert Morley—"BOAC takes good care of you"—except that the collar of his Van Heusen "stay-pressed" shirt is frayed; there is also a button missing on his sport coat. "Are you staying in the hotel?" he asks, lifting a tall glass of Tango punch.

"No. Have you heard of est?"

"I read an article about it," he said.

"Well, I was graduated from the training last week, and I'm here for the wrap-up, the lallapalooza." (The post-training.) "I'm on a ten-minute break," I said looking at the clock.

I had less than five minutes to go.

"By the way," he asked, "is it true that Werner Elgart was an encyclopedia salesman?"

"It's Werner Erhard, and I don't know. I've been told that he was in 'executive development.' Could be a euphemism, but—"

"Read it this morning," he piped in.

"Hey, listen, I have to get back."

Attempting to complete our conversation, I looked into his pale, watery eyes; they were the same color as cigar smoke.

"Did you 'get' it?" he asked, giggling, with his mouth over his drink.

"I'm not sure." I headed out of the bar and up to the second-floor balcony where the conference rooms are located.

As I entered the room, I saw Brendan chatting with a half-dozen graduates who were lolling about him.

"Should I hang loose with it?" one of the graduates asked.

"Hang loose with it and see 'what's so' for you," Brendan said. He was relaxed and at ease; with a glass in his hand, he would have made a good candidate for a magazine ad: "What does this man drink after a sixty-hour training? Dewar's."

Brendan received a signal from someone on the logistics team and turned from his admirers to shout, "OK, back in your seats. We're ready to begin."

The graduates followed his instructions, but slowly.

"Let's go! Let's go! We got a lot of ground to cover and I don't want to be here all night." The sound of his voice brought back traumatic memories of the training.

"The agreement is that you fill up the seats toward the front and center of the room first, and I don't want to see anybody positioning for the aisle," he said slipping back into his act.

"How do I know I got it?" he said, and the graduates responded with laughter. "Some of you got out of the training and felt better, and some of you got out of the training and felt worse. Does that mean you didn't get it? Some of you came out and you had these incredible realizations, and some of you came out and you didn't have any realizations at all. Does that mean you didn't get it? No."

The graduates chuckled again.

"How do I know I got it? Does it mean you woke up on the wrong side of bed?" Brendan could hardly contain his smile. "If you stopped smoking, does that mean you got it? No. If you started smoking, does it mean you didn't get it? Of course not.

"How do I know I got it? Does it mean you have to be able to see through walls? Does it mean you have to be able to walk through doors? No. It doesn't mean anything, and the interesting thing is that not knowing whether you got it or not doesn't tell you whether you got it or not."

Brendan re-created a story about a young boy who had stood up at the end of a teen training and said, "Well, nothing changed. I feel exactly the way I felt before I ever heard of est."

As he sat down, his mother raised her hand. "Wait a minute! Wait a minute! I've got to tell you, this kid is somebody else. He has been making his bed. He has been asking what he can do around the house. He even told me that he loved me. I don't know who he is anymore."

"So," Brendan said, drawing upon the example, "not knowing whether you got it or not doesn't tell you whether you got it or not; you'll be the last one to know.

"The only way you can say you got it is 'lyingly.' I mean, two months from now you can look back and say that your life is better or worse. All *that* is, is comparing the records. I want you to notice that.

"I want you to get that you can't compare how you are right now with how you are right now; there are no reference points, and how you are right *now* is the only thing that really matters experientially. All you can do is create a picture of how you think you were yesterday, and compare it to how you think you are now. And that's bullshit! It's a lie," he concluded.

In an interview I had run in the *East West Journal,* entitled "All I Can Do Is Lie," Erhard had said that when you put the truth into a system of comparisons, "it becomes a cradle for the lie.

"The only thing that isn't a lie," he said, "is your experience of what is happening right now! now! now!"

Brendan began the next part of his talk. "The purpose of the est training is to transform your ability to experience *living* so that the situations you have been trying to change, or put up with, clear up just in the process of life itself.

"By 'living' I mean right now; it's the ability to be in present time that keeps you from getting stuck in what happened. It's the ability to be in present time that determines how alive you are at any given moment, annnnd—you're going to notice that things do begin to clear up, just in the process of life itself.

"Now, you don't have to take any special pills to have that happen, annnd you all 'got' the training, and to accelerate the movement that you experienced in the training, Werner created the Graduate Seminar Program to continue to expand your ability to experience living.

"It's available to you, and it's not required. I'd like to stop here and have Tracy come up and talk to you about it.

"I think the world of Tracy," he said. "C'mon up here.!"

> clapclapclapclapclapclapclapclap
> clapclapclapclapclapclapclap
> clapclapclapclap

Tracy Goss is about five feet two and weighs in at about a hundred and fifty pounds. In her blue-flowered dress, cut low at her generous bust line, she is not unattractive or unappealing. She looks like a cherub of the holy order of seraphim (hybrid creatures who support and attend the divine throne). It is not hard to imagine Tracy with wings on her small back, and while I am not clear as to her relationship to the divine throne, she has spent the last two years as an attendant to Werner Erhard—close enough to the hot seat.

"Tracy," says Angelo Damelio, an est seminar leader, "is a very powerful woman." She has broken every record in the est stat book, including the enrollment of ninety-four percent of the people she is about to address in the Graduate Seminar Program. "Give her a job to do, and she'll get it done." One of the jobs that Tracy has done has been to bring est to Boston; and although my training, in April 1975, was the first to be held there, by October over two thousand people had enrolled in the training.

"Hi," Tracy said. She was all giggles.

"I'd like to tell you about the Graduate Seminar Program, which is available to graduates at a nominal cost." She was getting right down to business. The seminars go for thirty-five dollars apiece; they are ten to twelve sessions long and involve more expense to the est organization than the standard training. Pat Woodell, who is head of national enrollments at the est office in San Francisco, says that they are actually put on at a loss, and it is one of the reasons why the price of the training is as high as it is.

"Werner created the seminar series to accelerate the *movement* that you experienced in the training." It was a standard est rap, and Tracy played it back as if it had been prerecorded: "Please leave a message when you hear the beep." But underneath her mechanical repetition of the same old song was aliveness and enthusiasm. "I'm really very excited to tell you about it.

"Well," she said, her voice moving up a pitch, "I can see by the expression and color of your faces that you all experienced a lot of movement in the training." Giggle and titter.

The term "movement" is used in est to refer to those

things that may be set in motion as a result of taking the training, the process in which things begin to "clear up." As I can vouch from my own experience, the seminar series does tend to accelerate the speed at which that process takes place. According to an est brochure:

> Werner created the Graduate Seminar Program to provide an experience and a supportive environment from which graduates can come into the world, take responsibility for its condition, and experience and contribute to the expansion of love, health, happiness, and full self-expression through conscious participation, complete communication, acceptance of what is, and the willingness to take responsibility for their lives, est, and the universe.

The seminar series provide graduates with another opportunity to plug into the "safe space" of the training room and a seminar leader whose intention is to burn out their racket.

According to one seminar leader I talked to, "Getting the physical universe to work requires that graduates be willing to bring the 'safe space' of the training room into the world"—a process that requires cleaning up their own lives. To that end, there are processes given along with additional data, but these are tailored to "achieving a specific release or goal" by the end of each three-hour session.

The seminars are open only to est graduates; according to Brendan the graduates "are able to come into them without a mind."

There are six seminars offered.

"Let's see if I can remember them all," Tracy said, like a schoolgirl at a spelling bee. "There's 'Be Here Now,' 'What's So,' 'About Sex,' 'The Body,' 'Self-Expression'—oh, yes, and 'est and Life.' I guess that's it," she said proudly.

"Werner calls the series the Mastery of Life Series, so complete the series," she said (holding the proverbial carrot in front of a herd of donkeys), "and become a master of your own life."

"Question." Someone had raised a hand. "Yes, Kathy?"

"How long does it take to complete the series?" she asked, like a smartass indeed.

"About two years," Tracy said, pulling the carrot away, "and it usually works out that by the time you complete the series, Werner has created another seminar; he always manages to stay one step ahead of us. It also depends on the availability of the seminars you want to take in the city you live in.

"Boston is going to begin with the Be Here Now series, which you probably got some ideas about when Brendan was speaking earlier."

The est brochure on the Graduate Seminar Series says:

> The purpose of the Be Here Now Series is to expand your ability to experience being where you are—right now, with nothing added. Werner designed this series to enable you to move in the direction of experiencing life totally in present time—without the ceaseless chatter of your mind as it compares the way it is to the way it would, should, or could be.

"Another question?" Tracy asked, "OK, Clarence?"

"How many people are in each seminar?"

"They range from two hundred to two hundred and fifty; very much like the training," she replied.

"OK, question?" Tracy pointed to the back of the room.

Every time someone asked a question, Tracy would acknowledge the questioner with a series of rapid-fire motions: Drawing her right arm back toward her shoulder, she would let it fall like a karate chop, but would turn her wrist so it fell with her hand open.

The gesture seemed to contain both sides of her personality, and with it she could pick out her target with the accuracy of a radar-equipped surface-to-air missile.

"Staley?" she called out in a voice that always reminds me of one of Disney's Mouseketeers.

"Who will be leading the first seminar?"

"I don't know, but it will be someone who is specially trained by Werner."

Specially trained by Werner. This is the standard response to the question of who is going to be doing what and where in the est organization; the happy graduate learns to become non-attached. I once asked a person in the est office in New York, "Who cleans the bathrooms?" "Cinderella," he replied, "specially trained by Werner."

The seminar leaders are trained by Werner and by other heavies in the est organization over a period of two years. Compared to the trainers, with their enormous candlepower and high voltage, the seminar leaders (with some exceptions) are like fifty-watt bulbs.

I don't mean to imply by this that the seminars are not powerful experiences in themselves. "I now see my life in a totally new way," said one graduate at a seminar I later attended. "Uh-huh," said another, "so that's what the training was all about." "I've gotten it all over again," exclaimed a person who wasn't sure whether or not he really "got it" during the training.

"There's only one thing you do when you get it," Brendan said, "and that is to lose it. And that creates the space to get it again," clapping his hands rapidly, "a master is someone who's got it all the time."

Laughter!

Whatever their wattage, the seminar leaders are powerful people in their own right, and it is from their ranks that "trainer candidates" are drawn. Ultimately, it is not the identity of the leader of the seminar that produces the results; it is the willingness of the graduates to take the realizations and experiences that they have in est and make them work within their own lives. There are no guarantees.

"Are the seminars designed to help us solve the problems that didn't get solved in the training?" someone asked Tracy.

"They are designed to assist you in getting clear on what's so for you, now that you've taken the training, and—"

Brendan interrupted her from the back of the room. "The seminar program has been put together to continue to expand your ability to experience, with the intention that you be able to come from less and less of your machinery and more and more of you. You're gonna find that instead of being stuck solving the same old problems over and over again, you'll have some new ones to deal with; and when you solve those, you'll get some more; and when you solve those, you'll get some more.

"Life is a problem; and the solution to any problem contains the next problem that you are going to have to solve," Brendan said. "Sorry, Tracy, but I wanted to put that out there, and this was a good opportunity to do it."

"Thank you," Tracy said, welcoming the assistance.

"OK, if you have any other questions, hold them for now, and Brendan will deal with them later. Right now, what we're going to do is fill out a registration card for the seminar series. Look under your seats."

I picked up a small white card and a short yellow pencil.

"I'd like everyone to fill out a card, whether he's planning to enroll in a seminar or not," she went on. We were told this was for the purpose of keeping the records straight; those who didn't enroll that night would be called later.

The graduates completed their registration forms as if they were applications for Carte Blanche or American Express; they were careful to provide all the necessary information in their best penmanship.

"OK, now I would like you to all look over here," she said, pointing to the right side of the room, where a curtain was being drawn open in a herky, jerky way.

Voilà! The set was revealed as the curtain was fully

drawn: a long table with four graduates sitting behind it. On the table was a yellow sign with a brown border, and a couple of gray cash boxes. "Cashier."

We were given a ten minute break to write out our checks and "est money orders," which our banks would honor as legal tender.

I noticed during the break that the sales pitch, the cash boxes, and the money orders did not provoke the slightest note of cynicism amongst the graduates. An outsider might have said, "Well, they have all been *trained*, brainwashed"; but to me, as an inside outsider, it all seemed to be part of the game called est, and I enjoyed the opportunity to participate in it.

Brendan ended the evening with a process, and we all went home in a state of quiet exuberance.

It was all over, and it was only the beginning.

A Bite of the Big Apple

Shortly after the mid-training, I hopped a plane to New York City, one that was en route to California. I was dressed to perfection in a new pair of Bally shoes and a "trainer's shirt" of cotton knit, the French fit minus the epaulets, the true mark of the exalted ones. I would see other est graduates on this trip.

Werner has said that everyone who graduates from the training wants to become a trainer; what he does is create an obstacle course, and those who make it through, enter the ranks. I must admit to being no different from others in this regard, and by the time the stewardess told us we could go to the bathroom, I was headlong into my fantasy.

I walked carefully and gracefully up the aisle toward the bathroom. I was no longer your average writer on his way to the Big Apple; I was a trainer walking up the center aisle of a training room, and the people on either side of me were trainees.

Were they shaking in their seats? Did their apprehension mount as I walked by?

Probably not. They were headlong into their own whimsies. After all, they were important businessmen en route to New York and LA.

The big 707 tipped to begin its descent, and I stumbled to the bathroom door; it was locked. As I walked back to my seat, I thought of all the hours the trainers and seminar leaders spend on planes, and how that time might be well put to use in training the executive establishment of the American corporate state.

Adam Smith has written that est is like an American Airlines without any airplanes, and considering how much est spends on air travel, it might be a good idea if it were to merge with one of the big three. The advertising agencies would have a ball with it: "Fly United and 'get' est," or "Fly est and 'get' United." There are countless variations on the theme.

Upon arriving in New York City, I walked from the Port Authority terminal to the St. Regis Hotel, where I noticed the brass "cab call" between the subtle recessed twin entrances. The St. Regis, built by John Jacob Astor, is a unique survivor of the gilded age. Compared to its understated elegance, the Plaza is theatrical panache. I checked in and was escorted by an extremely polite bellhop to the eighteenth floor. I had more than three and a half hours before my first appointment, so I called the est office to see if there was anything going on in the city that I might participate in.

"Hello, this is Christa. How may I assist you?" asked a throaty voice.

I didn't say anything for a moment or two, thinking I had reached a massage parlor.

Christa said I was welcome to "assist."

Although the national est staff numbers over 200, most of the work—which includes addressing envelopes and calling people on the telephone to make sure they get their money in on time—is done by an army of unpaid volunteers.

"What do I have to know in order to assist?" I asked Christa.

"There is only one thing you need to know," she said, "and that is that you agree to get more value out of it than you put into it."

I took a cab down to the est office on West Thirteenth Street to get a look at the face behind the throaty voice.

Attached to the wrought-iron gate of an old brownstone was a pale-yellow sign with silver lettering: est. I climbed several flights of stairs, entered the office, and was immediately struck by how small it was. In this office, a converted apartment that according to the landlord measured no more than six hundred square feet, everything originated (until recently) that happened on the east coast of the est universe—in New York, Boston, Washington, and Chicago.

There were over thirty people busily milling around in it. Christa sat at a receptionist's table, greeting visitors between telephone calls. She wore wire-rimmed glasses, and with her curly blonde hair she looked like a kewpie doll.

"Hello, Robert," she welcomed me warmly, but in a slightly officious way.

"I'm here to assist," I said.

She asked me to write my name on a name tag, which I did somewhat nervously. "Now go down and see Rob in the basement. He'll be your assistance supervisor."

Rob was sitting at a small desk behind a pile of registration forms.

"I'm here to assist."

"Great," he said, smiling enthusiastically, "I'll set you right up."

The setup was that I was to put color-coded sticky round dots on registration forms that denoted who was going to be in what training.

"Use a red dot on the cards marked Graduate Review," Rob said, "an orange dot on the one marked October B, a silver dot for the Children's Training, and so on." There were about ten different categories, and after the registration cards were all color-coded, I was supposed to enter them on a Rolodex file and see Rob.

A simple task, but in a room that was the size of a freight elevator, there was so much going on that I found it exceedingly difficult to concentrate on what I was supposed to be doing. I caught myself putting silver stickies on cards marked Graduate Review and orange stickies on cards marked Children's Training. "*Be here now*," I said to myself, but I kept on making mistakes. I was distracted by every conversation in the room.

"Francine, did we get any yellow out?" Rob asked.

"Yeah, check bins number two and three," an attractive pear-shaped woman replied.

"It's not quite canary-yellow."

"It'll have to do."

"Did you sign me out on two books? Be Here Now, one and two," shouted Marvin through the din of voices; he had a black beard and a face like Nietzsche.

"Got it."

A man with silver-gray hair combed back over a bald spot walked over to my desk; he was about five foot three and fifty.

"Hello, my name is Lew Epstein. Who are you assisting?"

"I'm assisting Rob."

"Well, you know that if Rich comes down here and sees you without a name tag, its going to cost Rob some money," he said.

I had taken my coat off and with it my name tag.

"Rob can't afford that," Rob piped in. "It's already cost me twenty-five cents today."

"When did you graduate?" asked Lew.

"Recently," I replied.

"Well, you'll be up for parole in about a year," he said.

"What happens then?"

"A major transformation in your life takes place."

"Really? Tell me about it."

"Wait and see," Lew said and returned to his desk. "I got to call my insurance agent."

"Oh, look," someone said. "Here comes Brendan up the front steps."

"I think we should go out and genuflect and kiss his ass," Lew said as he dialed the number. "Hiya, Harold, this is Lew Epstein."

Harold must have asked him what he was doing.

"I've been working at est, leading graduate seminars so I can become a trainer candidate."

(What's that?)

"Eee-sss-ttt—Erhard Seminar Training."

(Never heard of it.)

"Well, we've had several articles written about us, some pro, some con, some good, some bad," Lew said. "It's been very gratifying."

(What's it about?)

"What happens is the mind dies."

(What? ? ? ? ?)

"I know what you're thinking Harold, and it's not that, so don't be alarmed," he said. "Listen Harold, do you think you'd like to take the training sometime?"

(No.)

"All right, I 'got' where you're coming from, what I want to talk to you about is transferring my policy."

Prior to coming to est Lew had sold over a million dollars worth of Israeli bonds; by the end of his conversation with his insurance agent, he had all but convinced him to take the training.

"I used to be a person who was afraid other people weren't going to like me," he said as he hung up the telephone. "I was cross-eyed and Jewish.

"The other night someone in my seminar stood up and

said, 'I hate you, I hate you,' and I gave him the space to do it.

"Later he came back and said, 'I love you.' It was beautiful," he said with his face in a glow.

I was more fascinated by Lew's candor than I had been by Christa's voice; he was a seminar leader on his way to becoming a trainer, and he was totally unpretentious. I respected him for it and told him so.

"Thank you, Robert, and thank you for participation in est."

I was ready to put the registration cards in the Rolodex. I had over a hundred ready to go, but the going was tough. I made more mistakes doing it than I had in attaching the color-coded sticky dots. It wasn't the menial nature of the task that was distracting me, nor was it my fascination with Lew; there were many things in my life that were still unresolved. I decided to sign up for the Be Here Now series as soon as I got back to Boston.

i. BE HERE NOW

I had experienced in the training that it was OK not to be OK, that things are perfect just the way they are, but not more than a week later, the all-knowing quality of the experience had become a mere concept. I was unwilling to accept that it was "OK" for certain relationships in my life to be unresolved; I was also unwilling to take responsibility for completing them. Murdering the alternatives, I buried them in the unconscious, but they rose up out of its internal mechanisms, and continued to run me like a machine.

It was producing a long chain of upsets, and every time I tried to pull away, I would only become more entangled in them. I was locked in and up tight.

Be Here Now, Number 1 was held at the Ramada Inn near Logan Airport in East Boston, and the seminar leader was Michael Rosenbaum, who had been second in command to David Norris during my training. Michael was dressed in a powder-blue blazer with gold buttons. He seemed ill at ease, but he had seemed ill at ease throughout the whole training; trying too hard to play his part.

Expressionless, he had walked around the room like a toy soldier that needed oiling. On several occasions, I looked at him and imagined a hidden battery pack within his chest. But along with the other graduates I welcomed him with unrestrained applause.

clapclapclapclapclapclapclapclap
clapclapclap
clap

"I'm very happy to be back in Bawston," he said in Brooklynese. "I'm really very excited about it. I love Bawston, and it's ninety degrees in New York."

Almost every est event I have ever attended began with "How happy I am to be back in Kalamazoo," followed by a comparison comment about the weather. "It's a hundred and ten in Afghanistan." I suppose Michael had to start somewhere, and the trickles of laughter seemed to put him at ease.

"In putting the Be Here Now series together, it was Werner's intention to create a space in which you can handle your upsets." It was our upsets that were keeping us from being in present time.

"Ever try to listen to someone when you were upset?" he asked rhetorically. "Remember how hard it was?" Michael told us that upsets are like old football injuries; the aches and pains are always there whether we choose to be conscious of them or not. He also told us that during this series all our recurring upsets were going to be "reactivated" and "experienced out."

"I know you don't believe that now," he said, "but stick around." He then asked the people on the logistics team to pass out the "Contract of Responsibilities for the Seminar Series"; it contained a long list of agreements that we were supposed to "make our own."

Michael read the contract out loud, emphasizing that we were to agree to attend all sessions no matter what came up; should an emergency arise, we agreed to call the est office and say that we would not be at our seminar. "At that time you agree to use the opportunity that you will be given by the person answering your call, to look at the space that is between you and your being there—and who put it there." But the agreement that seemed to offer by far the greatest possibility for practical application outside the seminar itself was number ten:

We were to agree to take care of whatever complaints we had by communicating them only to someone who had the power to do something about them. We were not to complain to anyone who couldn't do something about them.

"Choose the agreements, and particularly Number 10," Michael said, "and I can almost guarantee you that your life will work. Choose the agreements and you will not be at the effect of them. Choose the agreements so that you can choose to be here when you're here, and someplace else when you're someplace else. Choose the agreements and make them your own."

I did not have any trouble choosing the agreements, although I did miss a few sessions of the seminar. I "got" that the agreements were intended to support my being in the seminar and that my being in the seminar supported expansion and movement in my life. It was an easy choice to make, even though I knew that Number 10 was not going to be easy to put into practice.

Michael spent the next hour leading us in a discussion about the importance of bringing guests to the seminar with us each week; there would be a guest seminar held in another room in the hotel. It wasn't that we were under obligation to bring guests; it wasn't part of the contract;

it was just a strong suggestion, reflecting our willingness, we were told, to share our experience of the training. "It also reflects your ability to put something out there to people without getting in the way of them hearing it. In other words, it reflects where you're at."

Michael gave everyone the space to share his considerations about bringing guests, and then called a break. It wasn't until the second session that he began to deal with the substance of our upsets, and he began by passing out another sheet of paper on which was printed est's definition of an upset: "to overthrow or defeat, especially unexpectedly; to disturb the functioning, fulfillment, or completion of; to disturb mentally or emotionally." Michael added that upsets were usually caused by any one or a combination of the following: an undelivered communication, an unfulfilled expectation, or a thwarted intention.

It was clear to me that the chain of upsets I was experiencing as a result of my unresolved relationships with other people (some of whom were taking the seminar with me) were in themselves the result of "undelivered communications" on all sides. It was not clear to me, however, that it was my responsibility to complete those relationships by initiating communication, and that by not speaking to the other parties I "got to make them wrong."

"There is always a payoff in your upsets," Michael said, "or you wouldn't be stuck holding on to them." He invited us to share what our upsets were, handling each person who raised his hand by asking him what the payoff was. "Are you willing to let go of that?" he asked one woman who had walked out on her husband.

She was not.

"Do you 'get' that you are making a conscious decision to be upset?" he asked.

It was difficult to escape the pointedness and clarity of his questions, and it was not long before it became obvious that we were all choosing to be upset by whatever we were being upset by. There was always a payoff.

Several sessions later, he told us that in addition to our upsets being caused by undelivered communications, unfulfilled expectations, and thwarted intentions, they were aggravated by our tendency to generalize the finite into the infinite. "I want you to see that you have a finite number of upsets, and that they occur in certain locations at specific times."

Our homework was to list our ten reoccurring upsets, as well as to describe our experience of them in terms of "where, when, and what happened."

"What if we don't have ten?" a graduate asked.

"List all the ones you have. The purpose of the exercise is to see that they are finite; and be as specific as possible—where, when, what happened." He told us that we would use our list of reoccurring upsets during a process at the next meeting of the seminar.

In preparation for that process, he explained that the reoccurring nature of our upsets was the result of our being unwilling to experience and apply consciousness to them when they originally occurred. Using the piano stool he was sitting on as a symbol for our upsets, he began to demonstrate that we could hide from them, that we could attempt to walk away from them, that we could knock them over, or could even get down on the floor and play doormat; the point was that whatever we did, the stool would still be there.

"The only thing you can do when one of your upsets comes there is allow it to be there and apply consciousness to it," he said. "Whenever a problem, situation, or event in the immediate environment resembles the circumstances that led to one or more of the previous upsets in your stack," he said, "it pulls up all the others on a string."

The purpose of the process was to activate our previous upsets, to re-create them so we could "experience them out."

"Remember a time when you were terrified. Good. Re-create a time when you were alone. Great. Re-create a time when you were angry. Fine. Re-create a time when you were sad. Great." He then asked us to re-create one of our reoccurring upsets. "Allow it to be there. Take your fingers off the repress button. Notice any body sensations that are there. Notice any emotions that you are experiencing. Take a look at yourself and see if there are any attitudes involved, any thoughts or considerations.

"Recall the exact location where it occurred. OK.

"Recall what time it occurred. Good.

"What happened? Fine."

He told us to take a look at ourselves and notice any body sensations we were experiencing, emotions, attitudes, thoughts or considerations, images from the past; he gave us time to experience each category. "It's not going to get any better in here tonight; it's going to get worse." It was a long process, and it did not end until everyone in the room had completed his entire list of upsets, by re-creating them in the manner described.

During the process, I noticed certain reoccurring body sensations (a dull, aching sensation below the breastbone) in almost all my upsets. And every time Michael said to recall an attitude, I "got" that it was hopeless to struggle, accompanied by an image from the past. I was once grabbed by my shirt (underneath the breastbone), and taken into a cellar by a big black who tried to shove a piece of coal down my throat. Anger!!! By the end of the process I noticed that every time I got upset, it related to being told what to do, accompanied by a consideration that I had been backed up against a wall.

Michael had asked us during the process if we had made any decisions at the time that we experienced our upsets. It was almost too obvious: I had made a decision not to communicate with the people who upset me. Yet I was still upset about my unresolved relationships in the coming weeks, and lived with the constant reminder that I might eventually have to initiate communication on my own. And then a few days before Be Here Now session ten, I had a four-hour conversation with my wife as we drove from New York to Ogunquit, Maine, during which she helped me realize that the situation was "perfect" the way it was, that it was all right for things to be unresolved. I "got it." It came through to me so strongly that I was able to see that nothing had to happen in order for me to be satisfied in the situation.

Be Here Now session ten was pretty much the same as the previous sessions I had attended, at least in form. Michael led us through several processes in which we were told to re-create one of our reoccurring upsets: "If you get stuck, go back to a previously reoccurring upset." I went all the way back to being born—back, back, through my stack to the murder of six million Jews; back to the slaying of Christ; back, back, back back back to the embryonic stages of animal life and the evolutionary changes I had to go through in order to evolve and adapt to a changing environment.

"Get that it's OK for you to be upset." Michael said.

I not only "got" that it was OK to be upset, but that every upset I ever had contributed to the evolutionary expansion and movement in my life.

I don't know how or why it happened, but as soon as Michael told us we could go home for the evening, one of the people with whom I had been having trouble communicating sat down beside me and said, "I'd like to get together with you."

Be Here Now had worked.

ii. WHAT'S SO

The purpose of this series is to make it possible for you to become totally clear and responsible about your intentions in life. When you are clear about your intentions, you can communicate clearly and make agreements that are consistent with what you intend. As a result, things begin to turn out the way you said or thought they would.

Werner designed the series to support your ability to experience out the unconscious blocks and resistance to confronting the incomplete cycles in your life. This clears the space to realize what your intentions are or have been . . . so that life works.

—est brochure

I am tempted to say that I realized the purpose of the What's So seminar the moment I chose to take it. I read the passage in the est brochure, and asked what my intentions were. I had spent the summer gardening and sailing, and experiencing that satisfaction is not the result of what one does or achieves. It is the result of completion within oneself, and by the end of the summer I had completed what Lao-tsu calls "non-ado."

I was ready to get into something, and it was shortly after I enrolled in the seminar that I created the opportunity to write this book.

Session number one of the What's So series was held at the Sheraton Boston, in the same room where I had spent two days of the training. Tracy introduced Angelo Damelio, who was to be our seminar leader: "He's one of my favorite people." When I asked someone how to describe Angelo, he said, "as an angel." He may be an angel, but it is easier to picture him as a white-robed Roman senator with a Jersey accent in a Victor Mature movie. "Hay-el Caes-ah!"

Angelo is about five feet five, with short dark hair that hangs slightly over the Neapolitan collar of his checkered shirt. To use Angelo's own description of himself, he looks as if he had been run over by buses.

He is also cute.

Angelo passed out the Contract of Responsibilities,

stressing number ten as Michael had. He explained that he was an "optical illusion" and that there was nobody in the room to hear our complaints—they were merely our own projections.

"If you don't like the movie, don't fuck around with the screen," he said. "You know I'm such a Neanderthal that I actually used to do that; me and cousin Jerry and Billy and Johnnie used to go down to the movies and throw rotten eggs and tomatoes. Shows you the kind of guy I am."

    clapclapclapclapclapclapclapclap
      clapclapclapclap
        clap

"Thank you," he said. "OK, now that we've covered the ground of being on the agreements, let's talk about guests.

"First of all, I'd like to acknowledge everyone who brought guests tonight; please stand up," he said. About thirteen people stood.

    clapclapclapclapclapclap
      clapclapclap
       clapclap

"Now I'd like to acknowledge all those people who didn't bring guests tonight; please stand up."

    clapclapclapclap
      clapclap
        clap

"Thank you," he said. "You know when you people get over your resistance to bringing guests, you're going to find that your relationships with people are a lot better," he said. "You're going to rediscover people that you thought you'd lost.

"I had to go through an incredible amount of stuff to

push through my resistance to bringing guests. I created all kinds of barriers so that people wouldn't come; and one of those people is my cousin Jerry. He thinks I'm nuts. I created that, so now I don't get to play with cousin Jerry no more. Again, shows you the kind of guy I am," he said.

In the trainers, I had seen a proud humility; in Angelo, I saw a humble pride. It was entirely refreshing, and so was the What's So seminar. Although there were times when we would deal with some pretty heavy "blocks," Angelo always managed to keep them light. "It's my intention to make you so miserable in the seminar that when you get out of here you'll feel great!"

During the second session each of us was given a notebook. In it we were supposed to list all our incomplete cycles, by category.

"Working in your notebook is going to be one of the main processes we use in this seminar," Angelo said. He then told us to list each of several categories on a separate page.

"On the first page, at the top write 'Communications undelivered.' Skip a few pages; you'll need the space. On the next page at the top write, 'Things started and not being worked on.' OK" he said, giving us time to write a few of our incomplete cycles down. "On the next page write, 'Things being worked on and not completed.' Next page, 'Things I want to do presently and am not doing.' Next page, 'Things I wanted to have and don't have.'"

Angelo told us that since taking the What's So seminar himself, he had completed everything in his notebook except two catgories: "Things I wanted to have and don't have." He wanted a five-thousand-dollar camera—"and since I'm on staff" he said, "I'll probably never complete that." He had also written in his notebook that he wanted to become a trainer; he hadn't completed that one either, but I could sense that he was well on his way to doing so.

Our homework was to complete our notebooks. Angelo said, "Discount the undelivered communications that are easy to write down." It was those that we resisted writing down which were supposed to be of greatest value to us when we completed them.

"When I took this seminar, I didn't want anybody to see my notebook," he said. "Diane"—his wife—"would sneak up behind me and say, 'Can I see your notebook?' and I'd go solid." He told us that he kept his notebook hidden in his underwear drawer.

"By the time the next session comes around, if you still feel good about other people seeing your notebook," he said, "I'll know you didn't do your homework."

I completed my homework assignment during the next week, but on the evening of the next session, I noticed my notebook was sitting on my desk, where anyone could see it. Jesus, I said to myself, I'd better take another look. I sat down and came up with about twenty more undelivered communications. There was the motel room key in my desk drawer that I had intended to mail back over two years ago, and there were letters of thanks to former employers that I had been meaning to write for a long time.

I went to the next session convinced that I was not only aware of all my incomplete cycles, but well on my way to completing them. Angelo began the session by giving us about twenty more categories to write in our notebooks; and I went into a nose dive.

Crash!

My spirit started to rise when I noticed that my resistance to completing the new assignment came out of my resistance to completing the incomplete cycles it represented. I also noticed that Angelo was wearing a blue cotton shirt with epaulets, a trainer's shirt for sure, and a very costly one.

Angelo announced that he had become a trainer candidate, and the group rose with applause.

clapclapclapclapclapclap
clapclapclapclap

"It cost me thirty bucks," he said about his shirt. "But I've completed another incomplete cycle," he went on shyly. "And it's no more significant than the completion of anything else in my notebook." He was blushing.

clapclapclapclapclap
clapclapclap

"We say to complete one thing, anything," he said, "and when you've completed that, and experienced satisfaction, you will have created the space to complete something else."

Over the next month or so I was able to find many practical applications for this enormously practical suggestion. It was particularly useful to me in beginning my day's work behind the typewriter. One of the things that a writer has to deal with each day as he sits down to write is compressing the space of his thoughts and activities into an 8½-by-11-inch sheet of paper. It is like trying to walk through the eye of a needle, and one is apt to encounter a lot of resistance in taking the first step. On the morning that I sat down to write about the What's So seminar, I noticed that I was experiencing more than my usual resistance. I not only had to walk through the eye of the needle, I also had to pull the string of incomplete cycles along with me. This was a tremendous confrontation, but rather than begin my day in frustration, I chose to complete "one thing, anything," first.

Cynthia had asked me to fix the seat on my son's high chair, so I got out my tool box and cut a piece of leather to replace the caning, and in about twenty minutes it was done. I experienced so much satisfaction in accomplishing this simple task that when I returned to my desk, I was able to do so with a sense of completion, rather than a sense of having to complete something. In completing one thing, I had opened a wide space in the eye of the needle and I was able to slip through it like a silken thread.

I was told later in the day that my son had spilled about

a hundred of the quarter-inch thumb tacks that I had used in fixing the high chair. I stopped what I was doing and walked over to pick them up one at a time. It was like a little meditation, and in the midst of it I realized that in the process of completing the high chair, I had created another incomplete cycle by not putting the tacks away in the first place. I finished picking up the tacks and went back to my desk. As soon as I sat down, I "got it."

What I "got" was that in order to make life work, you don't have to have all your incomplete cycles completed; all you have to do is "complete one thing, anything," without creating more incomplete cycles than you can handle while playing the game. It's called winning.

iii. ABOUT SEX

The purpose of the About Sex series . . . is to allow you to locate and dissolve any barriers between you and communicating about sex. As Werner has pointed out, anything you can communicate about you can be with. This series is designed to expand your ability to experience yourself as the cause of your sexual experience, and not the effect.

—*est* brochure

During the period that I was taking the What's So series, I made an average of three trips a month to New York to attend other seminars and est events. On the twenty-fourth of October, I took a cab from the Souen restaurant on Ninety-second Street to the Commodore Hotel to attend Irving Bernstein's About Sex seminar. It was being held in the Grand Ballroom, only a few doors down from a spurious massage parlor known as Relaxation Plus.

Irving was in his early thirties. He wore a neatly trimmed black beard that seemed to accentuate his round face and cheerful smile. He was dressed as a CPA—his civilian occupation—not as a seminar leader or a trainer candidate; and he was able to lay down the ground rules with the simple eloquence of a Tevye.

To recap the purpose of the seminar: "The purpose of the About Sex series is to allow you to locate and dissolve the barriers to communicating about sex." Erhard has said that the essence of communication is intention, which means that when you communicate something to another person, you intend that he shall "get it." In order for him to "get it," you have to be able to re-create his point of view, and this in turn will create the space for him to be able to re-create yours.

Irving explained that, to that end, "long and boring processes" would be used in the seminar. "Yes, a question, Margot?"

"When you say that the processes will be long and boring," she said, "it makes me not want to choose the agreement to be here."

"OK," Irving exclaimed with a smile, "then the processes will be short and interesting—since it all comes out of your point of view anyway. You can have short ones, long ones, thick or thin ones. You're going to love the processes."

The seminarians cracked up over the double-entendres.

"There's going to be a lot of those," he said. "So be here and have some fun," he chirped. "Another question? OK, Sandra?"

"One of the barriers I'm really afraid to communicate about is the— I'm really scared to share this," she said, taking the microphone away from her mouth and resting it near her stomach. "I mean, I really am."

"Go on. Whatever you are unwilling to share, you are stuck with," Irving smiled, as he plunged into another sexual metaphor. "There's no cheese down that tunnel." Laughter.

She paused, and after a deep breath she released her secret. "All right, I don't have orgasms," Sandra said.

The room went into a hush, offering her a totally safe space.

"All right, you don't have orgasms. Are you willing to hang out with that for a little while?" Irving asked.

"I've been hanging out with it for a long time, so I guess I can for a little while longer." It was a moment of release.

"Good, thank you. I'd like to take a moment to acknowledge Sandra for sharing that," Irving said. "It took a lot of courage."

clapclapclapclapclapclapclap
clapclapclapclapclap
clapclap
clap

We were then led into a process in which we were asked to close our eyes and think of a reason for not communicating. "When you have one," Irving said, "keep your eyes closed and raise your hand until I call on you."

"All right, Bert?"

"They'll think I'm weird."

"OK, Janet?"

"They won't listen."

"Fine. Edward?"

"They won't think I'm a man."

It went on like that until about seventy-five people had given a reason for not communicating.

"One more," Irving said. "Lori?"

There were two women named Lori with their hands raised. They said exactly the same thing at exactly the same time: "Does it matter?"

Laughter.

"There are no accidents in the universe," Irving exclaimed, "and what matters is knowing that your reasons for not communicating are what's keeping you stuck in your relationships with other people."

clapclapclapclapclapclapclap
        clapclapclapclapclapclapclapclap
clapclap

Irving told us that pornographic films would be used during the processes of the later sessions, to assist us in handling what we were afraid to admit to ourselves about our sexuality. Angelo had mentioned these during the What's So series: "Whew! They are a tremendous confront."

One graduate I spoke to said, "I saw my first pornographic movie in the seminar, and while I was watching, I experienced a lot of resistance, and at the same time curiosity. It broke down a lot of my puritanical concepts about the way it should be done. Since then, I've felt much less resistance to enjoying myself, and more freedom in my sexual relationship with my husband."

They say in the training that life works on a set of rules. There has been so much said about sex elsewhere that I have condensed the observations I have made about it since taking the training down to a few simple statements. Remember, as Erhard says, there are no rules except one: "There are no rules."

The Seven Rules of Sex

ONE

We are each responsible for *creating* our own satisfaction.

TWO

By communicating what's so for us sexually, we create the space for a shared experience.

THREE

What we don't communicate with each other lies between us and experiencing satisfaction.

FOUR

Be willing to create it perfect the way it is; whatever you experience sexually is OK. Be at choice.

FIVE

Evaluations and judgments of sexual experiences do not increase satisfaction. If anything, they lessen it.

SIX

Don't use sex to go uneonscious about other things, and don't be unconscious during sex. Make love with the lights on.

SEVEN

All you have to know about sex is that "when you're hot, you're hot, and when you're not, you're not."

I once heard Werner Erhard asked a question about sex. His reply was, "Sex is the great involvement. And it may be that the only cure for it is old age. My own view is that we ought to lighten up about sex. We ought to allow ourselves to be as crazy about sex as we are."

iv. SELF-EXPRESSION

The purpose of the Self-Expression series is to expand your ability to express fully who you are. The seminars are designed to enable you to locate, communicate, and dissolve your notions about who you are afraid you are. What's left is who you really are—the source of your ability to communicate.

—*est* brochure

About six months prior to taking the est training, I attended a talk by Chogyam Trungpa Rinpoche, a Tibetan Buddhist master, on "Spiritual Materialism," the desire to grasp at the intangible. I had already read Trungpa's book by the same title, so I did not find the talk particularly interesting—besides which Trungpa was drunk.

I took to the question and answer period, however, as if Trungpa had secretly passed me a bottle of Dom Perignon. He would repeat each question as it was asked, but somehow he then always managed to formulate an entirely different question. The questions were comical but his answers were extraordinary; they were all right on target with the original inquiry.

"Right on!" shouted someone in the balcony.

It was an incredible Zen statement by Trungpa, and it goes to show that when we allow our essential Buddha nature to express itself, whatever we say is appropriate. It also goes to show that when we allow ourselves to get stuck in who we think we should, could or would be, whatever we say is inappropriate, at least if anyone's really listening.

Now Tibetan Buddhist masters are not concerned with who they should be even when they are drunk; they are who they are; but as far as the rest of us are concerned who we are is embarrassing so we usually pretend we are someone else. It is precisely that pretense, that mask, that lies between us and our innate ability to express ourselves.

According to one seminar leader I spoke to "self-expression is a function of taking responsibility for one's past." It is the shame and guilt that most people carry with them as a result of past misdeeds and unacknowledged actions that keep them stuck in what happened, and unable to express themselves freely in the present. "Responsibility," the seminar leader went on to say "begins with a simple acknowledgment that you are the cause of your own experience."

And acknowledgment is the key word in the self-expression series; when you can acknowledge all those things that you are afraid you are, and all those things that you are pretending to be, the only thing left is that you are.

And when you discover that you are, you also discover that who you are is the source of your ability to communicate.

In everyday terms, the self-expression series seems to be especially designed for those people who never know what to say, or are afraid of making asses out of themselves.

I spoke to several graduates of the series who said their ability to communicate had indeed been transformed, but the most interesting example I heard was given by Pat Woodell, head of est's national enrollment program, at a Special Guest Seminar in Boston.

> All my life I used to be a little shy, a lot shy. I was afraid to talk to people and to be who I was. In the training I got to find out what was behind that fear, during a process when we were asked to get in touch with an experience we had when we were five years old.
>
> I was brought up in Boston, and my mother was queen of the bargain hunters, and all of a sudden I was right in the middle of Filene's basement with my mother.
>
> It was very warm in the basement and I told my mother that I wanted to get a drink of water. She said OK, so I started out for the fountain in Filene's basement. I was having a good time playing with the water, and then I remembered I had to get back to my mother, and what happened was that I walked back in the wrong direction and got lost. I wanted to cry, but I was too embarrassed to express it.
>
> A lady came up to me and said "Are you lost?" and I was so petrified that I couldn't answer her.
>
> I sat there in a cold sweat, re-creating the experience, and I saw a decision that I had made when I was five years old, and that was that I would never allow myself to be put in another embarrassing situation like that;

and I realized that I had been operating off that decision for over twenty-four years.

So I got to be a shy little wallflower who was afraid to talk to people. And when I saw that, I started to laugh, and that fear started to dissolve, and I could be with people and express myself, being who I am.

Being who she is, Pat was able to share this story with over two thousand people, and yet all she had done was to re-create her experience in order to share it with other people.

One doesn't have to be as intelligent as Albert Einstein in order to say something worthwhile, or as well-informed as Walter Cronkite to be interesting; all one has to do is to get in touch with his experience and be willing to share it in such a way that other people can apply it to theirs. Communication is a shared experience of who you are, being who you are, shared with another person. As Erhard says, "What you say interests people; who you are inspires them."

Ultimately, it doesn't make any difference what you say. This was demonstrated to me at a graduation at which I assisted in New York.

Angelo was the training supervisor, and he was preparing a group of graduates to assist in conducting a "personality profile," an exercise in which graduates-to-be are asked to bring other persons into their "space" and say anything that they "see, sense, or feel" about their personalities.

In preparation for conducting the profile, Angelo led us into a process in which each of us was told to sit in front of another person, with our knees barely touching his, and recite a nursery rhyme, whatever one we chose.

"Mary had a little lamb, her fleece was white as snow," I recited to my partner, "and everywhere that Mary went—"

"How many people forgot the words?" Angelo asked.

About twenty people raised their hands.

"That's an acknowledgment to your partner," he said. "It means that he was able to create a space in which you could be with him more than with what you were trying to say. The rest of you," he burped, "got to be right.

"Now do it again, only this time, after each phrase, acknowledge that you got your partner's communication."

"Mary had a little lamb."

"Got it."

"Her fleece was white as snow."

"Fine."

"And everywhere that Mary went, the lamb was sure to go."

"It's the acknowledgment that you give to other people when they are communicating," Angelo said, "that creates the space for them to express themselves. It's not in the words, it's in the relationship that you bring into being." Jesus, that's important to get.

"Now, when you go into the training room to conduct the profile, I want you to know that whatever the person says is perfect. As long as a person is coming from his experience, whatever he says is perfect. It's just a question of accuracy."

In writing about self-expression, I am reminded of the conversations people used to have when they were high on LSD. The most circumstantial things they would say would reap replies of "That's perfect! That's it! Exxxactly!" It would go on like that, with double meanings on top of triple metaphors, until the only thing to say was that there was nothing to say.

Row, row, row your boat, life is but a dream.

V. THE BODY

The purpose of the Body series is to locate experience and dissolve areas of blocked consciousness in the body.

The processes, data, and exercises in this series are designed to enable you to move in the direction of experiencing your body as buoyant, radiant, and alive. . . .

—*est* brochure

Lew Epstein would be our seminar leader tonight. He was already sitting in front of the group when I walked into the Continental Room of the Statler Hilton to attend the body seminar. Good. During my previous visit to New York, Lew had pulled me over to a corner and counseled me: "Robert, you've just got to attend one of my seminars."

"So here we are, Lew," I said to myself. "I'm ready—and from the incandescent glow on your face, so are you."

Lew began the seminar by introducing the guests in the room to the training. He ran through the standard greeting, and invited them to participate in the guest seminar which would be held next door.

"I would like you to make it your purpose tonight to ask all your questions, and have them answered to your satisfaction, so that by the end of the evening you have enough information to make a choice about whether the est training is something that you would like to take . . .

"And remember, the est training is not an intellectual exercise or a concept but an experience.

"So in a minute I'm going to introduce your guest seminar leader for the evening. . . . Ivan, will you please stand up!"

Ivan was to be the first Boston graduate to lead a guest seminar, and the applause was long and loud.

```
clapclapclapclapclapclapclap
            clapclapclapclap
    clap
    clapclapclap
```

Ivan was the Raytheon executive who had stood at the door checking watches and timepieces. As the applause went on, Ivan stood in mute acknowledgment of it, with his eggshell head beaming under the lamp of good fellowship and approval. The applause stopped several minutes later, and Ivan led the guests out of the room with a bashful smile.

There was now only us—Lew and the body.

"Well," Lew began, "who would like to share?"

Jane stood up. She was tall, round in the hips, and in all ways lovely to look at.

"I have a great deal of uncertainty about whether I have breast cancer or not . . . and I recently had a biopsy . . . and they're still not sure."

Jane was not the only person in the seminar room who was uncertain about her body; as I looked around the room I saw many faces twisting in horror.

"Thank you for sharing that with us," Lew said. "OK, Sherry."

"Well, I want to talk about my hands. I am a pianist, and when I finished the training, I suddenly experienced my body and my mind flowing together in a way that they never had before. It was beautiful," she said, like a young Eleanor Roosevelt. "I was so happy. I was so complete . . . but then I lost that harmony. And now I want to create it again in the seminar here."

"Very nice, Sherry, very nice," Lew said. "What Sherry has done is share with all of us what life is all about—getting it, losing it, getting it. I want to tell you that there are no ultimate answers and that you can't hold onto anything."

Lew explained that the body is the sum total—"nothing more, nothing less"—of one's awareness: a linearly arranged, multi-sensory, total record of successive moments of now.

"OK, now let's do the first process. Uncross your arms and legs and take everything off your laps.

"Now focus all your attention on your left foot. Begin to untie the muscles in your left foot. If you wish, you may imagine that you are using your hands to do this, but don't do it physically. OK, now focus your attention on your right foot. Great. Bring your attention to your left knee and untie all the muscles in your right foot. Great. Bring your attention to your left knee and untie all the muscles in your left knee. Now—"

And on and on Lew went, leading us through the byways of our bodies: knee, thigh, chest, abdomen, chest, heart. I kept losing my awareness, going unconscious, and coming back. It was a forty-five minute process, and by the time it was over, I was still somewhere between my spleen and my pancreas, trying to untie knots and find out what was going on. Was there any purpose in this?

Lew must have been reading my thoughts. "There was a lot of unconsciousness in the room during that process," he said. "Well, that's OK, because after the break, we're going to do another process. What I want you to do is notice where you go unconscious. . . . By the way, the reason some of you can't get into your bodies is that you can't get out of your minds."

I spoke to one woman during the break who shared her experience of the process. When she reached the area of the left shoulder, where she had had a deep pain for years, she would go unconscious; that is, she would start thinking about what to make for dinner tomorrow or how to get the kids to the dentist. Lew's repeated command, "Get in touch with the left shoulder," triggered an image from the past. "I saw myself standing in front of a music stand with my violin gripped between my shoulder and my chin," she said. "I hated playing the violin. My father, a musician himself, expected me to practice for hours every day, and if I didn't, I would feel terribly guilty. The interesting thing is that as soon as I re-created that image, the pain went away."

I walked back into the room thinking about something I had read in the est brochure on the body. "Unconsciousness in the mind manifests as unconsciousness in the body. Tiredness, aches and pains, stiff postures are the result."

Lew began the second process. "Close your eyes and go

into your space. Notice a part of your body that you do not feel comfortable with. Notice how you are trying to avoid it by going unconscious. Notice that that pain or that discomfort is something *you* have put there. So now see if you can let it just be there."

The sharing began; and Bella, an attractive woman with middle-age spread around her torso, got up.

"Well, I don't have any complaints about my body. It doesn't hurt and I like it. I've never, ever, felt uncomfortable about my body. My mind gives me plenty of problems; my mind is crazy; but none of this ever seems to get into my body. I don't understand it, but my body feels terrific."

I sensed a hint of vanity in her noncomprehension. Lew cut in: "You say your mind is crazy and your body is fine. Terrific. Well, your body is the physical manifestation of your mind. That's all—nothing more or less. Your body is the physical manifestation of your mind."

Bella looked a little nonplused; she smiled and sat down.

I began to wonder what my body might have been trying to tell me during the alternating periods of consciousness and unconsciousness that I experienced in the process. Were they any different from the alternating periods of consciousness and unconsciousness that I had experienced outside the seminar room? Was my body the source of them all? Or was it my mind? I began struggling for a point of view.

"OK. Let's do the final process." Lew was still eager, and I noticed the contrast between the somewhat meek man with the thick, pilot-style glasses whom I had seen in New York and the gleaming, all-pervasive presence that now was on stage.

"Close your eyes, go into your space. OK. Now stand outside of your body. If you wish, put your body on a platform. Look at your body. Say hello to your body. Have your body acknowledge you. OK. Now have your body say hello to you. Now acknowledge your body saying hello to you. Great. . . ."

Lew continued with his instructions, but I was lost in what seemed to be an encounter with both my body and my mind. I was using my head to look at my body and my body to look at my mind. "Hello, body," I said to myself, and my body answered back, "Hello, mind." And then in this mutual acknowledgment something opened up in me and I realized that I was not my body, and that I was not my mind; and I experienced not having a point of view (as I had done in the training), and it was like "getting it" all over again.

I saw that what had happened in the training was that Erhard created a setting in which we began to realize that we were not our bodies; and as that happened, we also began to realize that we were not our minds. Lost in the universe without a point of view, we were able to experience ourselves wholly and totally.

Now the curious thing is that in order to experience this we had to be empty (no food) and we had to be clear (no thoughts) and we had to be opened up to realizing that whatever we apply consciousness to will start to disappear, including the aches and pains that we experience in our bodies.

And then it was over. Lew was as sharp about ending on time as he had been about beginning on time; but as I got up from my seat I experienced a sharp pain in the back of my head—and I was back in reality.

So reality is physical; there is nothing more real than pain, and the aches and pains that we experience in our bodies are an accurate indicator of our level of awareness, responsibility, and participation. The way to begin participating in our bodies is simply to notice what is going on. Notice where things are flowing smoothly, and observe those areas where you may be stuck.

As Erhard says:

"As long as a person is stuck in his body, no matter how high he tries to reach, he is held in place.

"The purpose of the Body series is to release the anchor."

vi. EST AND LIFE

The est and Life seminar is about getting the job done in life. Werner created this series to enable you to locate, communicate, and dissolve the barriers you have to getting the job done in specific areas of your life, including and not limited to your work. Getting the job done—making things go right, having them turn out perfectly—expands aliveness, creates space for people to experience, and produces the experience of completion, fulfillment, and satisfaction.

—*est* brochure

On a warm, sunny day in late October, I arrived at the old brownstone on West Thirteenth Street with the intention of interviewing Lew Epstein. I pulled on the brass door-handle, but the door was locked. "Where is everybody?"

I looked toward the basement entrance of the building, where a short, stocky man was emerging with a heavy can of trash. "Who you lookin for?" he asked in a grunt.

"est."

"They moved up to East Fortieth," he said shaking a fly away. "I used to be their landlord." He extended his hand. "Felice DeGregoria."

"Were they good tenants?"

"The best," he said, "Not a rotten apple in the bunch."

"Do you know anything about est?"

"All I know is that it made them happy," he replied amiably. "Whatever they did, it connected."

I took a cab to East Fortieth Street and was told by the doorman that the est office was located to the right of the building, on the second floor. I walked up two long flights of stairs that emerged into an expansive reception area with red brick walls.

Christa was talking to several people from the phone

company who were there to install an elaborate communications system.

"Hello, Robert," she said, handing me a name tag. "Please sign the register."

I opened a fire door to the left of Christa's desk which led into an L-shaped room about the size of a tennis court and a half. It was equipped with modern office furniture in Design Research style. Lew Epstein was on the phone and very much into a conversation, so I sat and tuned into the scene. It was the day after moving day, and the staff was scurrying around like a bunch of goldfish that had only recently been released into a thirty-gallon tank.

"Another year and this place will be too small for us," said a barrel-chested man with red hair and mustache. It was Rich Aikman, the new manager, the man who had tipped over the goldfish bowl to find himself floating around in an aquarium. "Angelo, get on the phone and call Jerry Joiner at the Ramada Inn in Boston," he commanded. "I want to talk to him right away. I also want to talk to Marvin, if he's there, and if he's not, find out where he is."

Ken, a tall, thin fellow in his early thirties who looked very much like a Presbyterian Danny Kaye, ambled up to Rich. "The room at the Plaza with the two bathrooms is not available," he said. Werner was due in town to have breakfast at the hotel with the New York staff.

"Those mother-fuckers," shouted Rich.

Ken smiled and in the streamlined accent of a Southern Californian said, "What is, is."

"OK, call San Francisco and find out what time Werner is arriving," Rich said. "I'd like to pick Werner up at the airport."

"What about the room at the Plaza?" Ken inquired.

"Who do those mother-fuckers think they are?" Rich bellowed again, only this time laughing. "We'll have to settle for another room."

My attention returned to Lew Epstein, still on the telephone. "I'm only telling you to take the charge off it," he said. He had been talking to the same person for over fifteen minutes. "See, your problem is that you refuse to get off it. . . . What? . . . I know you hate him, and you know what you are? A chicken-shit. Yeah, you're a chicken-shit," he said firmly. "You're afraid to talk to him."

On the opposite side of the room, gazing at a floor plan, sat Michael Rosenbaum. "Ange, can you go up to the hall and check on the security arrangements for the event?"

"That's nothing but your goddamn resistance," roared Rich from the other side of the office. "Address the envelopes."

"Hello, Jill, this is Angelo. I got to get in touch with Jerry Joiner." Jerry is a trainer. "Do you know where he is? . . . OK, I'll call back. Is Marvin there? . . . What the hell's he doin', buyin' a suit! . . . I've been disconnected!"

"Hey, Ange," Michael yelled out in a B-flat nasal, "you gotta get up there before one o'clock."

A woman picked up a telephone next to Lew and began dialing 225-5970. "Hello," she said, "this is Francine from est. I've got two machines I need installed today . . . No, I don't know what our account number is. OK, thank you."

Lew completed his conversation and welcomed me like a long-lost friend. I told him that I wanted to talk to him about his experience of est.

"Wonderful," he said. "We'll have to clear it with Rich."

Lew walked over to the door of Rich's office and knocked politely; then took me by the arm and led me in. A poster portrait of a roaring lion was taped against one of the walls. "Robert," Lew said, "you've created an incredible opportunity for yourself in being able to talk to Rich."

"Don't you have anything to do, Lew?" said Rich. "Wait outside."

I had been introduced as the person responsible for running the *East West Journal* interview with Werner Erhard.

"I really want to thank you for that," he said. "It's the best thing that's ever been done on us."

Given this complimentary introduction, I thought it was going to be all smooth sailing, that he would shortly let me talk to Lew about his experience of Werner and est.

"We've been told to refer all inquiries from the media to the est public information office in San Francisco. Are you in touch with the girl out there? What's her name?"

"Roxanne Curtis."

"Yeah, Roxanne."

"I'm in touch with Roxanne," I said, "and I'm also in touch with Arthur Crowley here in New York." Arthur works for a PR firm retained by est to play cat and/or mouse with the media.

"Did you tell them you wanted to talk to Lew?" Rich asked.

"No, I was in town over the weekend and couldn't reach them," I said. "I'd also like to talk to you."

"Well, you better get in touch with them. No, wait a minute," he said, "I'll call Roxanne." He dialed the number. "Hello, let me speak to Roxanne Curtis . . . She's on the phone? . . . Well, get her the hell off it," he said. "Damn those telephone men!" he roared. "This is the sixth time I've been cut off today." The line was dead.

Rich and I then began a twenty-minute conversation about whether or not he could talk to me. "Let me tell you something about how we operate around here," he said. "It's called 'agreement,' and the agreement is that I don't talk to you unless it is first cleared with Roxanne."

"I only want to ask you a couple of questions," I said.

"I don't care," he said. "You see this wall right here?" pounding his fist against it. "That's"—knock, knock—"what's so. It's solid, and the agreements in est are that solid. I keep my job by my willingness to keep my agreements and by making sure that other people on my turf keep theirs."

This agreement was a repress button of mine. In my previous attempts to talk to people on the est staff, I was invariably told to clear it with Roxanne Curtis, who told

167

me to clear it with Art Crowley, who told me he was going to have to clear it with someone in San Francisco, and whoever that person was, he was as invisible as Howard Hughes and equally reticent.

On the day that I walked into Rich's office, I had not been given a clear yes or no on any of these meetings, including an interview with Werner, which I had requested more than two months previously. And this was an organization that was in the business of communication.

"Now, as a graduate," Rich said pulling out a Rand McNally World Atlas from his desk drawer, "I am willing to share certain things about my experience of the training." It was the Catch-22 clause. "Tell me what you want to know and I'll see what I can do."

"How did you get into est, and what is your experience of Werner?" It was all I wanted to know in the first place.

"I used to be a sales manager for Redkin Cosmetics, and one day I knew it was finished—I had completed my work there—so I quit. A few months later I took the training, during which I got a lot more clear on the things I already knew. I also experienced my own perfection—you know, the same old story every graduate talks about."

Rich went on to say that after the training, he and his brother went to Africa to drive a truck across the continent, and every time he got to a town he would write Werner a postcard that said, "It's still working." After a month of "It's still working," he walked into a post office to pick up a money order and was told there was a letter for him. It was addressed, "Rich Aikman, Mozambique, Africa."

It was from Werner.

"It blew my mind! Not so much that he had written the letter, but that he was so clear on his intention that it actually got to me. I never told Werner where I was going to be. The only thing he could have known was my general route.

"When I got back, I attended a graduate seminar. Werner

walked in. There were two hundred and fifty people in the room. He had never met me. He walked right over to where I was sitting, as if I was an old friend, and shook my hand. I was so blown out that I asked Werner if I could volunteer some time to est. He said, 'Go see so-and-so tomorrow.' I asked him why. He looked at me with that smile of his and said, 'I know something you don't know.' The next day I was hired. Hey, let me call Roxanne."

Rich had a funny way about him. Several times during our conversation, he broke off to remind me about the importance of agreement; he was giving me everything I needed to know, but he knew how to push my buttons, as he did with everyone else.

"The line's still busy. I'm not going to tell you anything else until I talk to Roxanne."

Just then, Ken came in and told Rich that he had to deal with a disaster that had occurred in the office.

"Come back in two weeks and I'll have this place rolling. I'll have it rolling like an express train. Come back in three weeks and you'll see Werner out there in the machinery. It's all out there in my unrealized intention."

After Rich had left the office, Ken told me that Rich had been transferred here from San Francisco to give people a "direct experience" of dealing with someone in Werner's space. I knew what he meant. Underneath the lion's roar, there was a wise old owl and a pussycat.

Toward the end of my meeting with Rich, it had begun to dawn on me what "choosing the agreements" was all about; and that was certainty, the certainty of being able to win by playing by the rules of the game. I realized that in resisting the notion that Rich wouldn't talk to me unless I cleared it with Roxanne, I was alienating myself from being there with Rich. I also realized that it really didn't matter what Rich was saying to me; what mattered was my ability to experience what he was saying.

And suddenly, it was as if I were levitating above the whole scene, watching myself having a conversation with

Rich about whether he could talk to me or not. I started to laugh. By getting off my position, I was able to see our conversation from a higher level of reality. I was able to know that my role as a reporter was not to pry at people with can-opener questions, but to be there with them as an observer—an experiencer—of my own experience. As soon as I realized this I understood what it was to have a point of view and not be one's point of view. I also got that within every drop of experience is an ocean of knowledge; that what Rich had told me about the "agreements," was more valuable to me in getting the job done than anything else he could have told me about est.

Agreement: The act or fact of agreeing, or being in harmony; concurrence.

Agreeing: Consenting to; saying yes
being or going together, the absence of inconsistencies.

Concurrence: A coming together
a union in action
a meeting of minds.

While I was leaving the office, I heard Rich speaking to one of his staff members. "Hazel, don't give me any of your excuses; you have an agreement to get the job done!"

She started to blush. "Yes, I do."

"Then stay here until the job's done," he said, cracking a smile.

It seemed that Rich was being totally unreasonable, but by the time I stepped into my taxi, I woke up to the idea that the only way to handle the mind's reasons for not getting the job done was to have agreements. I began to realize how important it was, in the process of creating those agreements, to be clear on one's *purpose*.

In the est and Life series, "purpose" is defined this way:

Purpose: Intention or aim; direction; reason a thing exists. Goals change but purpose has a quality of being permanent.

Intention: The act or fact of intending; determination to do a specified thing or act. [Thought carries intentions as well as actions; some tennis players can influence the movement of a ball after it has left the racket.]

Note: Intention does not mean *trying* to get something done; it means *accepting responsibility* for getting it done.

Werner Erhard brought the est organization into being by taking care of all the little jobs that were right in front of him, with the purpose of *serving other people*. Out of this came a group of people who were willing to take over those jobs for him by making agreements to get them done as well as or better than Werner had done them himself.

Werner created the est Assistants Program out of the willingness of other people to support him giving them a way to participate in est. At an assistants' meeting I attended, Rich Aikman said to a group of people who were unsure whether they wanted to assist or not, "I want you to know that we don't need you to assist. Assisting is only a game that Werner has created to allow you to participate and bring the things you got out of the training into the level of daily life. I am also very clear that Werner doesn't need me or any members of the est staff; nor do I need him. I work for Werner because I enjoy sharing my life with him and playing the game called est, and in the process of playing that game and pushing through my own occasional resistance to doing the things I am asked to do, my life expands.

"The only thing that counts in business," he went on,

"providing you are ethical about what you do, is results. I guess that's about all; the only thing you have to know is that it is a game; you can make yourself miserable by resisting the agreements, or you can have fun by choosing them."

In spite of Rich's bulldozer tactics, it seemed that he had come close to mastering the game he was playing. He also seemed to have a great well of love in him—a quality that seems to be apparent in all masters of the game, whether they are in the business world, ashrams, or training rooms. To love is to serve.

I took a bus back to Boston; and in the process of cleaning my study dug out an old est newsletter; on the back page was a short essay written by Werner. It was entitled "Taking the Mystery Out of Mastery."

> Mastery of life comes from the ability to create a game and stay centered as you play it out.
>
> Life is always perfect just the way it is. When you realize that, then no matter how strongly it may appear to be otherwise, you know that whatever is happening right now will turn out all right. Knowing this, you are in a position to begin mastering life.
>
> In order to master life, this is what you have to know: Life is a game. To have a game, something has to be more important than something else. There is nothing which is intrinsically more important than any other thing. Importances are created by agreement alone. To have a game, "where you are not" has to be more important than "where you are." You decide or agree to what's important, then begin to move or flow toward it.
>
> There are three things that affect your ability to get directly to where you want to be: co-flows, cross-flows, and counter-flows. Co-flows push from behind, cross-flows push from the side, and counter-flows push head on. If you think that a co-, cross-, or counter-flow is going to stop you, you may want to stop to handle it.

However, the only thing that really stops you is stopping to stop another flow.

To get from where you are to where you want to be, just acknowledge that the flow is there and expand your purposes to include it. In other words, make it part of your purpose for the other flows to get where they want to go.

Playing the game of life so that you come out on top at the expense of others is beating the game. Playing so that everyone succeeds is mastering life.

Chapter VIII

THE WIZARD OF est

"Werner is going to be giving an all-day seminar on Making Relationships Work next week," Angelo said at our What's So seminar. "Anyone who wants to form a car pool to San Francisco, meet in the back of the room during the break." Laughter! "Let's see, from Boston it should take you about four and a half days. That is if you don't stop to eat."

The car pool didn't pan out, but after the break, an enthusiastic seminarian suggested that we all fly out to the Golden Gate by rent-a-plane. Only three days and a couple of all-night vigils later, the est office in Boston had successfully chartered a Boeing 707, and filled it with over 170 people from all over the East Coast. "It's called 'flying intention,'" one graduate remarked as I arrived at the airport. "It's really 'getting it' up there."

"How long will the trip take?" I asked a bag checker from the friendly skies of United Airlines.

"Four and a half hours flying time, depending on the head winds," he said. "Your plane is leaving from gate eleven."

It was about twenty minutes past one, and the plane was scheduled to depart at two A.M. I hustled down the glistening corridors, and after a pit stop X ray at the weapons detection unit, I could see my sleepless comrades in the distance; they were floating over the polished tiles like a mirage.

I hustled down the ramp toward the gate; they were calling my name and applauding. "Right out of *Juliet of the Spirits*," I said, reaching the dock.

"Present from Werner," said Ole, a Dutch guest seminar leader, with twinkling eyes.

Jill Richards took a corsage out of a large, flat rectangular box and handed it to me. "Present from Werner."

Tracy Goss, who had worked long hours to put the whole thing together, came rolling down the ramp. She picked up a telephone to call New York. "Boston is all checked in."

We boarded the plane a half hour ahead of schedule, and the stewardesses couldn't handle the fact that we were all wearing name tags. "Are you planning to hold a convention at thirty-three thousand feet?" I was asked by a well-put-together blonde with a southern accent. "It'll be close to three o'clock in the morning before we leave New York."

I told her that we were in the business of manufacturing altimeters, and that a convention would be perfectly appropriate, but "As for myself," I said, "I plan to get some sleep."

"You won't get any sleep on this flight," she said.

As the plane lifted off the runway and began circling over Boston Harbor, I looked down at the disappearing lights of the city; I imagined they were thousands of tiny stars in a dark but viscous space. I drifted off as the plane flew deeper into the universe, over and across the Bay State.

"OK, everybody, wake up." It was Mary Tess, a petite and always effervescent graduate with a Peter Pan face and a pixie haircut. She was speaking over the plane's public address system. "Reach down and pick up the song sheet below your seats," she said. "Don't peek in the white boxes." They were the kind of boxes bakery goods are packed in; each was tied with a gold string. "OK. I'll sing it through once, and then the rest of you will join in."

It was a welcome song for the graduates whom we would pick up at La Guardia, and it was sung to the tune "Hello, Dolly."

Well, hello, New York
Well, hello, DC
It's so nice to have you all on board the plane.

You're looking swell New York
You're looking swell DC
Cause we're all getting off on playing Werner's game.

This trip was so outrageous
and we knew we'd do it,
Cause we're all clear on where we want to be.

So hello to San Francisco,
you're really only just a stone's throw.
Werner, we're coming out to play.
We wouldn't have it any other way.
Werner, we're coming out to be with you today.

      clapclapclapclapclap
           clapclap
               clap

I resisted singing the first two renditions, but by the time the plane touched ground in New York, I was standing in the aisles, opening my arms like Satchmo in the final refrain: "Werner, we're coming out to be with you today."

The additional passengers were greeted with a practiced congeniality; as the stewardess had told me, it was close to three A.M. before we were airborne again, and still no sleep.

I had tried to position myself so I could sit next to an attractive woman—someone on whose shoulder I could lean my head during the long night—but I had gotten so carried away singing Mary Tess's song and pretending I was Mitch Miller leading the Army Air Corps Glee Club that I almost wound up without a seat. Manuel Manga, an old friend with the imagination of the Monkey King, had seen my plight and invited me to take an empty seat in his section.

He was sitting next to Ann Gordon, a curvaceous brunette who happened to be an assistant dean at MIT; he would lean on her right shoulder and I would lean on her left; before long we were all curled up around each other in a human knot, and sleeping as soundly as could be expected.

I woke about an hour later, and found people flirting with each other in the aisles and sipping cocktails.

The bakery boxes had been opened, "presents from Werner"; they contained an array of fruits, nuts, and imported cheeses on a bed of shredded yellow cellophane.

I nudged Ann's head gently over on to Manuel's shoulder and got up to take a walk; I walked past a pretty blonde wearing the tightest possible denim pants, with double diagonal zippers on each of her hips.

She stopped me by looking into my eyes. "You have a lovely face," she said.

I smiled from ear to ear.

"What do you do?" she asked.

I told her what I did. "What do you do?" I asked knowing that it's the kind of question that sometimes makes it impossible for people to tell you who they are.

"I'm a television producer." Her name was Barbara.

Someone walked by and offered us a piece of birthday cake; she accepted, I declined. "Would you like to sit down?" I asked.

"Sure," she said seductively.

It was going beautifully, except that we couldn't find a

place to sit, and when we did, it turned out to be someone else's nest.

"Hey, Robert!" It was Lew Epstein calling me from the back of the plane. "C'mon back here."

I used it as an opportunity to get out of a possibly awkward situation. "Excuse me," I said. "Talk to you later."

I walked back to where Lew was sitting.

"Robert, I've been thinking about you. You're the only person on board this plane with a reason for being here. The rest of us are here because we're crazy."

In my writing about est, there had been many occasions when I found myself looking at my experience over my own shoulder, but this wasn't one of them. "I'm on this plane for the same reason everyone else is—to see Werner," I said, "and I don't have to fly to California at one o'clock in the morning to know I'm crazy."

We both laughed.

I ambled back toward my seat, stuck my foot in the magazine pocket, and went to sleep.

I woke up about an hour later when my foot broke through the pocket; it was a little after five A.M., a good time to go for another walk.

A pale green glow of phosphorescent light was being emitted from the instrument panel in the plane's cockpit, but the passenger cabin was dark and quiet. It was as if I had dozed off and awakened in an enchanted dwelling high above the earth. I took each step slowly, being careful to look at each person's face as I passed by. I looked at them in the way I look at the faces of my children when they are still and asleep.

I reached the cabin and poked my head in the door.

The captain turned around and said, "How you doin', buddy?" in a gentle voice. He was a 'good ole boy' out of Memphis. "We're doin real fine up here."

I told him I was having a "high flight." I was so energized by the love I was experiencing that my body seemed weightless, rather than heavy for lack of sleep; it was as if I were being suspended by an invisible skyhook an inch or two off the cabin floor. I said good night and returned to my seat.

Ann woke up as I sat down, and asked if she could put her head on my lap.

I said it would be fine.

So she put her head down.

And I circled my arms over her with the intention of creating a circuit to transmit the peace I was feeling.

The next thing I heard was an electronic "dingdong."

"This is the captain speaking.

"We'll be arriving in San Francisco in a little less than an hour.

"The weather is clear, a cool sixty degrees.

"I can't tell you how much we've enjoyed having you with us tonight." It was no longer the routine speech. "And maybe we can all spend some time together when we get to San Francisco."

       clapclapclapclapclapclapclap
          clapclapclapclapclapclap
  clapclapclap
      clap

"He doesn't know it yet," said a graduate across the aisle, "but he wants to enroll."

Shortly before the plane touched ground, we were each given an envelope; it contained a small white card printed in old English lettering:

"I am moved by your support. I am inviting you to attend a party with me after the event at Polk Hall." It was signed, "Love, Werner."

* * *

The plane landed about seven-thirty A.M.

We were greeted by a squad of est staff members and

whisked by bus to San Francisco's Civic Auditorium, where the event, Making Relationships Work II, was to be held.

The Civic Auditorium is located between Polk, Grove, Larkin, and McAllister Streets. It is a massive building; behind its Greek facade are four stories of meeting rooms and an auditorium that sits squarely in the center of the building like the huge belly of a Sumi wrestler.

We were ushered through the cavernous reception area and up into the balcony, where a special section had been reserved for those of us who had come from Boston, New York, and as far away as Tokyo. I sat where I could lean over the brass railing of the balcony and get a better look at what was going on down on the main floor prior to the happening.

Resting my elbows on the railing, I began to take in the auditorium. It was a large, semicircular room with squared sides, like part of an octagon. About three hundred feet away from where I was sitting was an expansive T-shaped stage. It was covered with a dark-blue carpet that matched a dark-blue one-hundred-foot curtain hung at the back of the stage. Approximately twenty feet to the left and right of the stage were two large movie screens (fifteen by twenty feet) upon which Werner Erhard's image was to be recreated by live video to provide a more intimate atmosphere.

As my eyes wandered around the auditorium, I noticed a small room about eighty feet off the floor, to the right of the T. It was the light room. There were four men standing in it; in the distance they looked like tiny statues that had been carved into a hole in the wall.

A large carousel of lights hung from the ceiling like an upside-down birthday cake with its candles lit; it illuminated the main floor, where thousands of people were in the process of either locating or holding onto their seats. The sections were broken up into rectangular areas of portable chairs, 150 to each section.

Over six thousand people were attending the event; and

they squirmed in their seats like an army of astronauts making last-minute checks on their equipment. On Werner's arrival, they would be rocketed into their space.

To an observer, the lift-off might appear to be slow and precarious, but inside the tiny capsules of their minds, the G force would mount rapidly during the processes, as if under a million pounds of thrust. It would increase their mental speed until they broke through the barriers to experiencing their relationships as complete. Once they were in orbit, there would no longer be a question of their survival; having released their minds like Saturn V boosters, they would release their burden of "being right."

I looked at my watch. It was eight-thirty, and the event wasn't scheduled to begin until nine A.M.

In preparing to leave for California, I had not had the time to look at the biographical material on Werner sent by est the day before. I had brought it with me to the event, so I opened it and read it while I was waiting. It was a twelve-hundred-word mimeographed biography, the only information that est had provided me during the entire time I was writing this book. It had taken me seventy days, nine letters, and thirty phone calls to get a straight answer to my request for an interview with Werner. Finally, in response to a detailed list of questions I sent to Werner and Roxanne Curtis, I had been sent this poop sheet.

It was the kind of stuff passed out by your social studies teacher—as if you didn't know who was buried in Grant's tomb. Written in Grolier Encyclopedia style, it was as dull as a butter knife and as sketchy as a sand painting. I looked at the letter Roxanne had sent with it: "It should answer any of your questions." It answered none of them, and created a lot more. What was the big secret?

Using the bits and pieces it provided and background material I had compiled from various sources, I was later able to eke out a biographical sketch of my own:

Leaving Philly in 1960, in the company of a woman named Ellen (whom he was later to marry), Werner took a plane to St. Louis. It was during this flight that he changed his name from Jack Rosenberg to Werner Erhard. "My mother was a very strong woman, and my uncle was a captain in the police department, so I wanted a name as far away from John Paul Rosenberg as I could get." It was during his stay in St. Louis that he began his career in educational publications, selling the Great Books for Brittanica.

He left St. Louis and moved west to join the sales department of a matchbook correspondence school, selling courses to people who indicated they were interested; as one writer put it, "like a good est graduate today." He moved to Spokane, Washington, in 1961 and began studying a wide variety of disciplines, among them Scientology and hypnosis. He also studied at the Dale Carnegie Institute, applying the things he had learned in these courses to his business career.

In 1963, he went to work for the Parents' Cultural Institute and made his mark training door-to-door encyclopedia salesmen. According to his boss at PCI, "He was hired because he had a reputation for honesty and integrity, and an ability to develop effective programs." So successful was he at this that he was later moved up to vice-president. Asked by the *East West Journal* what his role was, he replied, "I was doing executive development and motivation, and my job was to work with people in such a way that productivity increased, leadership increased, and executive ability increased; and that's what I did."

Dale Carnegie was only one of the techniques he used; he synthesized the techniques of Maxwell Moltz, the American Management Association, Industrial Psychology, and PACE. But it was the more esoteric disciplines he added to the pot that made his approach unusual. He was a "discipline freak," and he subjected himself to every discipline he could find, participating at various levels, from student to instructor. One day Werner told his boss that he was going to use Zen on the sales force, and his boss said, "Great. Don't get any on the walls."

Whether or not Werner was successful in using Zen on the sales force at PCI is hard to determine, because the company folded in 1969. Erhard moved on to work for Grolier's; its business was selling encyclopedias as well as other educational publications. In addition to supervising a large number of sales people, he continued his work in executive development, concentrating on middle and upper management. Asked if these programs led to his initiating est, Werner replied that they had to a certain extent. "Because business is the only place where you can move around from discipline to discipline. Business doesn't care what you do as long as it isn't blatantly illegal and it produces results." But in order for him to produce those results he had to recognize the trappings of the disciplines he was involved in and drop them. "I had to separate the bullshit from the gunsmoke."

It was out of a synthesis of Werner's past that est was born, and out of the "enlightenment experience" he had. "I was driving across the Golden Gate Bridge one morning on my way to work, and I saw everything I had ever done, and why it worked, and why it didn't work. I saw why all of the disciplines worked and why none of them worked. And it was in this state of total clarity that I realized my life wasn't working and that I was the cause of it all."

Immediately after this experience, whatever he did "worked"; and a month later, in October 1971, he got up to do the original est training.

Of all the influences in Werner's background that went into creating est, he has said that Zen was the most powerful. Other significant ones were Subud, Gestalt, Encounter, Mind Dynamics, and Scientology. It was from Mind Dynamics, according to Alexander Everett (its founder), that Werner "got the whole idea of the 'personality profile,' the 'processes,' and 'going into your space.'" It was from Scientology and other psychological disciplines that much of the data evolved. It was the experience on the Golden Gate Bridge, however, that gave him the "critical mass of insight" that allowed him to throw all the pieces of the puzzle up in the air and pick them up again as Erhard Seminar Training.

The est organization emerged as the framework around the puzzle, and Werner's background in business as the bulwark of the organization's rapid expansion. While other trainings were isolated, at hidden retreats in the mountains of California or the deserts of Mexico, Werner was able to bring the training to thousands of people throughout the country with a singular skill: his ability to motivate other people. The "source," as the people in the organization like to call him, is a supersalesman; and according to Rich Aikman, he used to bend people's arms to get them to take the training. Since the early days, however, he has changed his approach; he now tells people that he isn't interested in "selling them" on taking the training, but more than that, he tells them that they "don't need the training." Combining the two most important elements in his experience, I wound up with the "Zen of Salesmanship" or "How to Succeed in Business without Really Trying."

I still had a great many unanswered questions about Werner Erhard and the est organization, not the least of which was the organization's unwillingness to communicate; but at this point, the mimeographed biography was as far as I could pursue them. I put it back in my school bag and began observing the people around me. On my right and left were two middle-aged housewives from Marin and Sonoma Counties; one was twiddling her hair, and the other was chewing gum and playing with the clasp on her pocketbook. Although any group of sixty-five hundred people obviously must contain a diverse cross section of persons, the two women sitting on either side of me seemed to represent perfectly that cross section which is always particularly conspicuous at est events—middle-class whites.

They were people who for the most part had enjoyed such a relatively high degree of material success that they had all but given up on the idea that "more is better."

The last time I'd been to the Civic Auditorium, it was to attend the Kohoutek Celebration of Consciousness in 1974, an event so plugged into the system of "more is better" that it was patently ridiculous.

Touted as "an alchemical mix for transmitting individual approaches to the new art and science of consciousness," it turned out to be an indigestible recipe for enlightenment. As Theodore Roszak has described the event:

> If one searched out all the booths and all the workshops in all corners of the auditorium, one came upon Palmistry, and the Tarot, Witches' Rune Sticks, Practical Divination, Manifest Wisdom of the Great Pyramid, Cosmogenic Art . . . The Life of Maharaji on Film, Bio-Magnetic Psyches for Insight, Past Life Readings, UFO Research, Electro-acupuncture, Chaotic Meditation, Tantric Healing, Shiatsu, Parapsychology for the Business Executive, ESP, Teaching Machines, Orgasmic Union, Pathways Vibrations, Karma cleaning . . . Universal Bio-Imagery . . . One Psychic Development Counselor advised all comers to "Expect a Miracle Today, for There Will be Many"; another featured a "Self-Liberation Karma Buster," made of genuine plastic and selling for only one dollar.

At the Kohoutek Celebration of Consciousness, it had taken the promise of more, more is better to entice people into the corridors of the building where most of the events were held; except for a sudden rush of seekers brought on by the occasional appearance of the Mantric Sunband, or the Cosmic Beam Orchestra, the center was empty. A year later, it took only the presence of one man to fill the auditorium, to center the energy, and to give the event a single purpose: Making Relationships Work.

One of the most confusing things about Kohoutek was

the wide variety of terminology used to describe an equally wide variety of subjective experiences; it was like the tower of Babel; instead of a "meeting of the ways," it turned out to be a battle of semantics: "My guru is better than your guru."

Some people, like Roszak, went home to begin charting the map of the "Aquarian Frontier"; others, like Erhard, recognized the need to define their terms before entering into the arena of the human potential movement. Where Kohoutek had spread and scattered its light like an illusive rainbow, Werner Erhard, ex-used car salesman, meat packer, and construction supervisor, had somehow recaptured it in a single beam. Cutting through the confusion in an era in which so many became lost in the search for consciousness, he brought thousands together in shared experience with the laser-like clarity of his intention and a Webster's dictionary.

"Hi, I'm Werner Erhard." He had made his entrance.

```
        clapclapclapclapclapclapclap
                    clap
              clapclapclapclapclap
        whistles
                        clap         clapclap
                 clapclap
```

His face flashed on the video screens. "Thank you."

```
         clapclapclapclapclapclap
                clapclap
                        clapclap
                                  whistles
                     clap
```

"Thank you."
The audience was cheering wildly.

clapclapclapclap
　　　　　　　clapclap
　　clap
　　　　clap

"Thank you." He motioned them to sit down.

They did so reluctantly, lingering in the euphoria of his climactic entry into their space.

It was exciting to see Werner's giant image appear on the video screen and to see him alive on stage at the same time. His appearance was perfect; he was dressed with great care down to the last detail. Custom-tailored light beige slacks, a brown crewneck sweater accented by the open collar of his blue shirt, which give him that California casual look. Everything is "appropriate." Everything about his appearance "works"! The blue collar blends with the darker blue draperies that extend to the ceiling behind him. Thus, he and his physical space harmonize, each becoming an extension of the other. Werner's presence is alive in the auditorium itself.

He thanked us for our presence; then established the purpose of the event in terms of what he didn't want to accomplish: he didn't want to make our relationships get better, he didn't want to send us out with some tools to use to try to make our relationships work, or to give us another set of considerations that were superior to the ones we already had.

His voice enveloped the auditorium like the resonating percussion of the Zarathustra Symphony.

He wanted, he proclaimed, nothing less than a complete transformation, an alteration of substance, not merely a change in form.

Thus 'spake' Werner.

If we could confront and be with a transmutation in our relationships, he went on, that's what would be accomplished here.

It was in this moment that I crossed through the landscape of my imagination, the hours spent in precognition of the event, and entered into the reality of the actual experience. Into the inert substance of my preconceptions came the mystic prana that would innervate my pulse beat for the next twelve hours.

The purpose of Making Relationships Work, he explained, was to give us the opportunity to handle what might be blocking us from completing relationships, and to discover what we could do to complete our relationships so that they could begin. And our being there, he said, was a total validation that our relationships weren't working.

I was a bit taken back; my purpose in being there was to be with Werner. Like most of the other people in the room, I would have been there if he was giving an all day course in do-it-yourself auto repairs. I did begin to realize, however, that here was an opportunity to make my relationship with Werner work.

He began reading a prepared text thanking us for allowing him to assist us in making our relationships work and inviting us to relax and to enjoy ourselves. There might be times, he warned, when resistance would come up from what we were doing. He urged us to let it be when it came up, whether it was annoyance, negative judgments, sleepiness, upsets, sadness . . . No matter what came up, we were to be absolutely willing to let it be. Whatever we could let be would allow us to be, and that was the beginning of mastery.

In allowing the things in your relationship to be, he explained, and in allowing yourself to be, you take the struggle out of living; you begin to recognize that the most important thing in your life is that you are, and that the most important thing in your relationships is that you are in relationship. I recalled the Graduate Event in New York at which Werner described the single experience out of which Making Relationships Work came into being. It was an experience that was very powerful for him, and it was born out of trying very hard at making his relationships not work. He said that one day he woke up and realized that he didn't have to work at making his relationships work. The most fundamental fact of his existence other than that he was living was the fact that he was related.

According to what Werner was saying about MRW, out of the discovery that you are related comes the impulse to experience completion in your relationships. Therefore, when you talk about allowing things to be, you're talking about experiencing things as deeply and as fully and as intimately as you possibly can. So he wanted us to create as much space, as much room for things to come up as we possibly could, and to expand our space to include whatever we might pick up about people out there. Whatever you can allow to be allows you to be, he reminded us—and the whole purpose of our being there was to allow ourselves to be in our relationships.

It seems to be Werner's particular genius to allow himself to be in relationship with thousands of people whom he has never met. It also seems to be his particular genius to be able to bring those people into relationship with each other. He asked us to stand and instructed the light crew to turn up the dimmers. He wanted us to expand our space to include the event, he said. He told us to expand our space out through the walls of the auditorium, out to the streets on all sides of the building, the auditorium, out to the streets on all sides of the building, out to the sky above it and the earth below it. Now, he said, he wanted us to take a look at the people inside our space, at the cameras and electronics there, and at all the other people inside our space. He wanted us to get the idea that we created this space, to give ourselves the chance to make our relationships work.

He asked us to look around the room—as evidence of a very strong intention on our parts.

laughter

>   clapclapclapclapclapclap
>   clapclap
>   clapclapclapclapclap
>   clapclap
>   clap

Then he directed the people on my side of the balcony to say hello to the people on the other side of the orchestra, and vice versa.

"HELLLLLLLLLLLLLLLLLLLLOOOOOO!" the balcony roared.

"HELLLLLLLLLLLLLLLLLLLLLLOOOOOOO!"

>   clapclapclapclapclapclapclap
>   clapclap
>   clapclapclapclapclap

I had held out on the first greeting. I had come three thousand miles to be with Werner. I wanted to sit down with him over a couple of beers and talk about the Millennium the way Norman Mailer would talk to Muhammad Ali about prize fighting—no bullshit, just plain talk. Instead of a quiet bar or meeting place, I had wound up in a crowded auditorium with over six thousand people. On the second call, however, I let go of my resistance to being there, and shouted, "Hellooooooo!" I began to realize that allowing the other people—including some of whom I had experienced as obstacles within est—to be in the auditorium with me, allowed me to be in the auditorium with my own experience. I saw that there was an opportunity there to re-create Werner's space, to relate to the thousands of other people as deeply and fully and intimately as he seemed to be relating to them.

Perched over the music stand, he peered into the crowd like a falcon. His head turned from side to side, while his clear blue eyes scanned the total space of the auditorium. It was as if he were noticing each person, even in the extremities of the room; yet he never seemed to focus on any one individual. [His styled brown hair, neatly combed back off his brow, frames the sharp features of his face; a prominent nose, sensuous lips, and a mouthful of perfect teeth. He is usually smiling.]

He was into the next phase of the course. He began constructing the launch pad upon which the event would be hurled into space with a discussion of definitions. (We had been given a long list of them as we entered the auditorium.) The purpose of going over these terms was to become absolutely clear on what it is that we were here to do—because, strangely enough, all a person has to do is be clear on his intentions in order to have those intentions realized spontaneously.

He gave us a little background:

All his life he had thought that he actually had to work on things to make them happen; as a matter of fact, he actually taught people how to make things happen. It was only in the last few years that he discovered that simply knowing things in a way that allows them to happen, allows them to happen. In other words, what causes something to happen is not what you do to make it happen, but the way in which you know what you want to happen. In order to know something so that it can happen spontaneously, it is essential to become really clear about your terms. Thus the value of our going over the list.

He predicted that in going over the definitions, we would have realizations, or "mind states," when the light goes on. He said we should allow it to go on, but keep on going—you won't want to get stuck in enlightenment.

Laughter!

For the first time since Werner had appeared in the auditorium, the screens hung vacant of his likeness. I watched him move on the T-shaped stage. He is about 5'8", trim but husky, presenting every bit of his body; there is not even a fallen shoulder or a tired slouch. He is not holding onto anything in a posture. Even in the way he carries himself across the stage, one can see the clarity of his intention. Like a Japanese Noh dancer, he moves with total consciousness of his body moving through space, and it looks natural and unassuming.

He broached the first word: "making."

A group of definitions appeared on the bottom half of the screen; no esoterica here. They were mostly drawn from Webster's dictionary, "making" a lot of good sense.

Though many of the elements of Werner's teachings are discussed in books such as the *Upanishads,* the *Bhagavad Gita,* and the *Tibetan Book of the Dead,* he has not relied upon them for his vocabulary. He has, instead, relied upon and taken responsibility for the words that are endemic to our culture, sometimes to the extent of being grievously pedestrian. And that's precisely the point; in this way he has been able to communicate the experience of est to over seventy thousand people. One need never have attended a lecture at the Esalen Institute, or taken an introductory course in suburban Yoga to be able to get est's message.

The two platinum-blonde middle-class housewives sitting on either side of me had their eyes glued to the video, as if they were contestants on a T.V. game show.

making
1. bringing into being; specifically,
    a) causing; bringing about, producing
    b) form by shaping...

Most of the words he was using to define "making" had more to do with *being* than *doing*: it's important to understand, he pointed out, that making relationships work doesn't necessarily imply *doing* anything. "Making Relationships Work" involves looking inside the box that we keep our relationships in, and seeing that they actually do work. And in order to do that, we were going to have to see what a relationship is: he made a distinction between a "relationship" as a being aware of and understanding of another persons way of being, and what he called "involvements," and "entanglements."

People who are related often get the idea that they are involved, he said, and the involvement may be shoving the relationship out of the way. To be "involved" in a relationship means—back to the dictionary again—"to make intricate tangled or complicated . . ."

Laughter!

"Involve," he explained means "to require, to make busy, or to occupy"; to a lot of people it means taking up your time because they have nothing better to do—and that's an involvement, not a relationship.

"Entanglement," he went on, is another good way of looking at what we're not talking about. "To entangle" means "to catch, as in a net, or vine [etc.] so that escape is difficult."

Laughter!

He added that if you've got an entanglement and you refer to it as a relationship, you've made a whopping error!

Laughter!

It was amazing how you could describe most people's relationships right out of the dictionary.

Occasionally, he lets out a self-amused giggle; it borders between a slight note of sarcasm, and compassionate wisdom. He looks handsome one moment, and rather plain the next. In successive moments of now, his radiance expands and contracts like a luminous star; the light goes on and he smiles, he smiles and the light goes on in the corner of his eyes. "Integrity," says Werner, "is that which produces the greatest amount of aliveness." In those moments when the light is on, his aliveness speaks for itself, and one must assume his integrity.

Werner said that satisfaction in any area of life starts with telling the truth. The truth was that I was involved and entangled with him professionally, yet underneath that involvement and entanglement there was also a relationship. It was out of that relationship that I was experiencing expanding satisfaction and aliveness. So rather than allow myself to be ensnared in the net of uncertainties that hung over me like a huge question mark, I began to take a look at the ways in which my relationship with Werner was actually working.

One of the most obvious was that my relationships with other people had improved considerably as a result of my participation in est. I noticed it first in my marriage; it had undergone a long series of ups and downs prior to my taking the training, but by the time I boarded the plane for the Golden Gate, both my wife and I could say to each other in complete honesty that we were wholly satisfied in our relationship. It was as open and alive as a spring flower coming up through the cleanest snow; each time I saw her it was like meeting a new person, to whom I was intensely attracted. Upon arriving at the event in San Francisco, I had already experienced that "a relationship doesn't begin until it's complete"; I was complete in this one, and in many others.

On top of this, there were many other things that demonstrated that my relationship with Werner was working. I was more centered, more self-confident, and more in command of things that came up. I was not easily upset. I was able to take things lightly and philosophically. I had completed many incomplete cycles. I needed less sleep, less food, less approval—and my sense of well-being no longer depended on the agreement of others. I was healthier, more energized, and no longer caught up in the need to achieve or prove myself. I was able to get whatever job I was doing, done—with more satisfaction and without creating more incomplete cycles in the process. I was more at ease in potentially embarrassing situations. I was more honest, ethical, and embracive of others. I was able to acknowledge them in ways in which I had never been able to acknowledge them in the past. I was able to love them, to accept them for what they were and for what they were not. I experienced more space in my life, more room to move around in, and in that space I was beginning to play around with the imagination and inventiveness of a child. In all those ways and more that are too numerous to mention, my relationship with Werner was working.

And the most interesting part of it was that I had no personal involvement with him. So I began to see Werner in an entirely new way—not only as a personality who could be captured in images and later transferred into linear removable type, but as someone who had come to represent the potential unfoldment of the seed of perfection within all of us. I saw him as someone who had transcended normal identification as a personality and come to personify the "self that we call the self." Werner was becoming larger than the events he was participating in or creating. In other words, I began to perceive him as a mythic being, someone whose self-conceived mythopoeiac destiny was to "get the physical universe to work."

Whatever part his personality had to play in that course of events, the events themselves, like MRW, had become the enactment, the sustaining element behind both the myth and the nuclear society that was being organized around it, the est organization.

* * *

Werner called a bathroom break, and I got up from my seat wondering what the implications of his being God in the est universe were. As long as he was willing to acknowledge that I was God in my universe, it seemed perfectly OK. Still, he was the one with the expanding organization that obeyed his every command. Whatever was going on—or had the possibility of going on—at the interface between his universe and mine, I wanted to know about; and I suspected that a lot of other people wanted to know about it too.

As I walked out of the bathroom, I was distracted by a group of est volunteers who were entering to see that all was in order.

There were always many people who were willing to support Werner, willing to re-create his space, even within the unglamorous setting of a public toilet. The platoon of volunteers I had seen entering would demonstrate the same sense of responsibility that I had seen the trainers demonstrate in the training room; they would not leave until the results were produced, until the space they had been entrusted with was entirely clean.

As a member of a society that has all but buried the myth of the Protestant ethic, I couldn't help but wonder why they were so willing to work. Was there a new "Werner Work Ethic" emerging? Was it based on the promise of expanding satisfaction and aliveness in the now? Or were these merely acts of redemption for all the things that happen or ever happened that Werner said they were responsible for?

Whatever their motivations were, the event was running like clockwork, and I had already experienced tremendous value out of my participation in it.

"We're about to begin," shouted one est volunteer, who was obviously having a good time. "Please return to your seats. We're about to begin."

I scurried back to my seat, and the event resumed exactly on schedule.

Werner led us into a process. "Take everything off your laps, and get into a process posture."

Laughter!

I was tired by this time—I had not slept more than an hour on the plane—so that when given the opportunity to close my eyes and go into my space, I went directly to sleep. I woke up a few minutes later with my head bobbing.

Werner was saying, "What would have to disappear in order for your relationship to be complete?"

"The est organization," I said to myself.

In my relationship with Werner, the incompletion I experienced seemed to come out of my relationship to the est organization.

"What would have to disappear in order for your relationship to be complete?" he asked again. "Choose that as your item."

I saw the organization as a barrier and Werner the

source of the barrier in the same way that he is the source of the organization.

"How do you use that item to make yourself right and the other person wrong?"

It was true. I used the unwillingness of the est organization to communicate with me as a way of making Werner wrong.

I settle back in my seat, and begin daydreaming; I am soon asleep again. I wake up a few minutes later with my chin nodding into my collarbone. With my eyes still shut, I raise my head up quickly, as if I am trying to pull in a big catfish.

A midair transformation occurs; in raising my head, I see the est organization arranged in space like a three-dimensional spiral hologram of an atom.

It appears that all the energy in the spiral is moving toward the center; as it moves down the spiral's track, it becomes increasingly *one-pointed*, reaching its maximum intensity as it enters the nucleus, Werner's space. (It is being given an intention.) Werner then takes it and channels it back out through a series of electrons: the trainers, the seminar leaders, the graduates. And almost everyone who comes into contact with it begins to get in touch with his own power.

Out of the spiral image and out of my own experience of the est organization—which I had come to see as the personification of its source—I was able to make certain observations about Werner. The most obvious one was that he can be unreasonable in his intentions and loving in his embraciveness—abrasive and embracive in the same instance.

"I am big, I have many contradictions," said Whitman. The thought of Werner Erhard's being a man of contradictions did not come as a surprise to me. Powerful people are usually contradictory; it is one of the things that makes them so powerful. It was in the expansion of my point of view toward the end of the process that I was able to see why Werner had chosen the physical universe as his guru, and see—in the simplest terms—how the physical universe worked.

> The physical universe is the master, the guru
>   a master is someone who found out,
>   a disciple is someone who listens
>   to the master because
>   the master's life works.

> The physical universe does only One thing,
>   it expands and creates space,
>   and in the space that it creates
>   things come into being.

> Werner Erhard is the master's disciple,
>   and in the est universe
>   he only does One thing
>   he expands and creates space
>   and in the space that he creates
>   things come into being.

> Some of the things that the physical universe brings
>   into being are galaxies, stars, and planets
>   on those planets, man comes into being
>   with the unique capacity to experience
>   his own beingness.

> Man also comes into being with a mind or ego
>   that attempts to survive,
>   by dominating other beings
>   or by avoiding being dominated by them.

> The mind gets stuck in its point of view,
>   the soap opera or drama of the specific
>   circumstances it is involved in
>   the mind always identifies with the body
>   or piece.

Werner created a space where the mind stops
> thinking it is the being,
>> where the mind stops
>>> thinking it is the body,
>>>> where the mind stops
>>>>> thinking it is its emotions,
>>>>>> where the mind stops.

And the being comes into being
> the master
>> expands and creates space.

I opened my eyes and looked at the large video screen, and once again I saw the "movie" of Werner. I experienced my mind popping on as if the picture had set off a burglar alarm in a vaulted silence. Jack Rosenberg, alias Werner Erhard. I was out to get the man who had taken money from these unsuspecting people at $40 a head, a man who had conned over sixty-five thousand others into paying him $250 each to "get" nothing but a punch line to a cosmic joke. "He had to be the greatest, subtlest con man who ever lived," and my mind kept on running its number. It was out to dominate this man, in a cold-war game of survival. I watched it and played the game at the same time, and at the same time I knew that I was not the game.

I experienced Werner with both my mind and my being, and in the polarization of those opposite experiences I realized that here was a man with a mind involved in the game of survival, in the same way that anyone's mind is—perhaps not to the same extent, but in the same way.

I sat there as if suspended over the entire auditorium waiting for the scenario to play itself out. And it came down to this: Werner had been given a great deal of power; was he using that power responsibly?

* * *

Werner led us through a long series of processes and then called a lunch break. I scooted out of the auditorium and into the California sunshine, and bought a couple of oranges in a Chinese grocery store on Market Street. I had planned on taking a cab to the Franklin House, a Victorian mansion behind whose locked doors Werner usually holds court, but there were no cabs around. Instead, I decided to shop for a present to bring back to my children. Walking up Polk Street and down McAllister, I saw a small bookstore tucked into a quiet side street. I went inside and browsed through the children's section, where a big W caught my eye . . . *The Wizard of Oz.* Then I thought, "Werner, the Wizard of est!" I leafed through the familiar classic and began reading. Here is my own abridged and paraphrased version of what I read:

> The four travelers passed a sleepless night, and the next morning a soldier came and took them into the Throne Room of the Great Oz. Presently, they heard a voice that seemed to come from near the top of the dome.
>
> "I am Oz, the Great and Terrible. Why do you seek me?"
>
> "Where are you?" they asked.
>
> "I am everywhere," answered the Voice, "but to the eyes of common mortals I am invisible."
>
> "We have come to claim our promise, O Oz," Dorothy said.
>
> "What promise?" asked Oz.
>
> "You promised to send me back to Kansas," said the girl.
>
> "You promised to give me brains," said the Scarecrow.
>
> "And you promised to give me a heart," said the Tin Woodman.
>
> "And you promised to give me courage," said the Cowardly Lion.
>
> "Well give me time to think it over," the Wizard said.
>
> "We shan't wait," said Dorothy, "the Wicked Witch is dead."

The Lion thought it might be as well to frighten the Wizard, so he gave a large, loud roar, which was so fierce and dreadful that Toto jumped away from him and tipped over a screen that stood in a corner. As it fell with a crash, they looked that way, and the next moment they were filled with wonder. For they saw, standing in just the spot the screen had hidden, a little old man, with a bald head and wrinkled face, who seemed to be as much surprised as they were.

"Who are you?" the Tin Woodman cried out.

"I am Oz the Great and the Terrible," said the little man.

Our friends looked at him in surprise and dismay.

"I thought Oz was a great Head," said Dorothy.

"I thought Oz was a lovely Lady," said the Scarecrow.

"And I thought Oz was a terrible Beast," said the Tin Woodman.

"And I thought Oz was a Ball of Fire," exclaimed the Lion.

"No, you are all wrong," said the little man meekly. "I have been making believe."

"Making believe!" cried Dorothy. "Are you not a great Wizard?"

"Hush, my dear," he said. "Or you will be overheard— and I should be ruined. I'm supposed to be a Great Wizard."

"And aren't you?" she asked.

"Not a bit of it, my dear; I'm just a common man."

"You're more than that," said the Scarecrow, in a grieved tone, "you're a humbug."

"Exactly so!" declared the little man rubbing his hands together as if it pleased him. "I am a humbug."

"Really," said the Scarecrow, "you ought to be ashamed of yourself for being such a humbug."

"I am—I certainly am," answered the little man sorrowfully; "but it was the only thing I could do. Sit down, please, and I'll tell you my story."

"I was born in Omaha—"

"Why that isn't very far from Kansas!" cried Dorothy.

"When I grew up I became a ventriloquist, and at that time I was very well trained by a great master. I can imitate any kind of bird or beast," he said. "After a time I tired of that and became a balloonist."

"What is that?" asked Dorothy.

"A man who goes up in a cloud on circus day, so as to draw a crowd of people together and get them to pay to see the circus," he explained. "Well, one day I went up in a balloon, and the ropes got twisted so that I couldn't come down again. I traveled high above the clouds and on the morning of the second day I awoke in a strange and beautiful country."

"It came down gradually, and I was not hurt a bit. But I found myself in the midst of a strange people, who, seeing me come down from the clouds, thought I was a great Wizard. Of course I let them think so, because they were afraid of me and promised to do anything I wished."

"I ordered them to build this City, and my Palace; and they did it willingly and well. Then I thought, as this country was so green and beautiful, I would call it the Emerald City, and to make the name fit better I put green spectacles on the people so that everything they saw was green."

"But isn't everything here green?" asked Dorothy.

"No more than in any other city," replied Oz. "I have been good to the people here and they like me; but ever since this Palace was built I have shut myself up and would not see any of them."

"I think you are a very bad man," said Dorothy.

"Oh no my dear; I'm a very good man; but I'm a very bad Wizard, I must admit."

"Can't you give me brains?" asked the Scarecrow.

"I can stuff your head full of brains, but you don't need them. You are learning something every day. A baby has brains but it doesn't know much. *Experience* is the only thing that brings knowledge, and the longer you are on earth the more experience you are sure to get."

"But how about my courage?" asked the Lion anxiously.

"You have plenty of courage, I am sure," answered Oz. "There is no living thing that is not afraid when it faces danger. True courage is in facing danger when you are afraid, and that kind of courage you have in plenty."

"How about my heart?" asked the Tin Woodman.

"Why, as for that," answered Oz, "I think you are wrong to want a heart. It makes most people unhappy. If you only knew it, you are in luck not to have a heart."

"And now," said Dorothy "How am I going to get back to Kansas?"

"We shall have to think about that; in the meantime, you are welcome to stay here. There is only one thing I ask in return. You must keep my secret and tell no one I am a humbug."

They agreed to say nothing, and went back to their rooms in high spirits; even Dorothy was willing to forgive him everything.

Oz, left to himself, smiled to think that he had given the Scarecrow, and the Tin Woodman, and the Lion exactly what they thought they wanted. "How can I help being a humbug?"

I closed the book with a big chuckle!

While the Wizard had made promises that he could not keep, Werner always came through on his. The only thing I had ever heard him promise was what was already so. "What is is and what ain't ain't."

I gave another chuckle, purchased the book, and started walking back toward the auditorium.

I was an hour early, so I sat down in the park across the street. It was alive with mums, evergreens, yogis, sidewalk musicians, and est graduates. I stretched out in the sun and began thinking about my relationship with Werner.

Was there anything left to complete?

I still hadn't talked to him about the millennium, the way Norman Mailer would talk to Muhammad Ali about prize-fighting.

I looked across the street; there was a platoon from the est volunteer army's maintenance division heading my way.

They were carrying cardboard boxes and chanting, "The event is about to begin." They were going to clean the park.

"That's what you call taking responsibility for the physical universe," I said as I crossed the street to return to the auditorium.

I showed my reentry pass and entered the building. Climbing the stairs to the balcony, I chose a new seat near one of the microphones. Sitting next to me was a young woman with short, straw-blonde hair and granny glasses who worked as an assistant computer operator in an insurance company.

We got into a conversation, and she shared with me that she was having intimate relations with three men and didn't feel complete in any of them.

I looked her in the eye and said, "Three's a crowd."

Werner returned to the stage and proceeded to complete Making Relationships Work. In the next process he opened the space for everyone to experience what it would be like to complete a relationship. He was adept in his game, and he seemed to have an intuitive awareness of the space everyone in the room would be in at this point.

We were told to open our eyes and come out of our space, stand up and stretch. "Good!" he encouraged us. Then he talked us back into our space, for another process. When the processes were over, he told us that it was time to do some "acknowledging."

An "acknowledgment," according to Webster's is an expression of thanks, often for something you've been keeping a secret.

And one of the most valuable things I had learned in est was the importance of acknowledging people. But it was at this point in the event that I realized that in acknowledging another person's way of being, I was also acknowledging my relationship with them; saying in essence, "It's working."

Werner is a master of acknowledgment and if I had to pick a single reason for the est organization's working, this would be it: he really knows how to appreciate people, and he never keeps his appreciation a secret.

There is always an atmosphere of celebration around Werner, and the second part of the event was no exception.

It was in the expanding joy of that celebration that I was able to experience being complete in my relationship to thousands of people I had never known, and to others I had known only too well.

He began by expanding the acknowledgments to those people who were *not* involved here in the auditorium today; because, as he pointed out, what's going on in the auditorium is very much representative of what's going on in the world: there's a whole group of people who don't know that they're a part of est, but whose interest and way of being support est and the things that it represents. He asked us to assist him in acknowledging them.

> clapclapclapclapclapclapclap   clapclap
>   clapclapclapclapclapclapclap
>   clapclap
>   clap

I thought of all those people who out of the basic impulse to share their experience, and out of a basic commitment to the world's enlightenment, had allowed the consciousness of this planet to expand. I looked back at all the groups and gurus and plastic karma busters that had participated in Kouhoutek, and saw how they had all supported me; not only by creating a social context in which an event of this size could occur, but by their reading of those publications through which I had come into contact with est.

It was through my entry into the spiritual supermarket that I realized that smart shopping, as Rinpoche says, does not involve collecting a lot of information, but a true appreciation of each individual object. I was able to truly appreciate est because there were no trappings around it; like a polished stone, it had an earthy elegance about it that was irresistible; this in itself was an acknowledgment to the star-studded setting of Werner Erhard and the space that he had created for people to support him.

The next group of people to receive acknowledgment were those thousands of people who in assisting in est have made est work, while expanding the quality of their own existence and making a qualitative contribution to society.

clapclapclapclapclapclapclap
clapclapclapclap
clapclap

I began to get in touch with the experience I had of the people who had assisted in my original training, and it was one of sheer awe. Sixty hours, a long-distance marathon run with the microphones; why did they do it? They did it out of gratitude to Werner, to be sure, but more than that they did it out of love, and the willingness to go through all the inconveniences involved in sharing that experience which had been of ultimate value to them.

The est staff was next—those people who create the space in which est takes place and evolves. Werner made an incisive point about the way people who see themselves as "serving" are often stuck in sacrifice, fanaticism, and righteousness. So he especially wanted to thank the est staff for getting the job done and for getting it done out of joy, inspiration, aliveness and integrity . . . He asked us to assist him in acknowledging them.

clapclapclapclapclap
clapclapclapclap
clapclap

Although I had experienced a long chain of upsets in dealing with the est organization's "righteousness and fanaticism," it was through Werner's acknowledgment that I realized I had also experienced its "joy and integrity." It was through my own acknowledgement that I knew it was possible to be complete in relationships in which there were cross flows and counter flows. Letting the past be, not getting stuck in "what happened," I was then able to re-create Werner's experience of his own staff. It was in the space that it had provided me that I was able to get whatever value I had created in est. It was also in that same space that I would be able to share that value with other people.

"You don't have any idea how good it feels to acknowledge people," we had been told in one of the graduate seminars.

I was beginning to get the idea.

It was with the intention of acknowledging those things in our past that we were "stuck on" that Werner led us into a process in which he asked us to *let go* of the past. Whatever happened or was supposed to have happened, he said, "Let it be."

One of the things that was supposed to have happened in my past was the opportunity to talk to Werner about est and the year 2000. When the process was over, he gave a little talk about completing the past, and I was able to put the millennium into its proper place.

What he said was that you can't create the future except right now. He drew two lines on the blackboard, calling one the future and the other the past, in between was the present. He walked away from the blackboard and confronted us with some hard facts: The only place you can work is in the present-right now. All that talk about the future is a waste of time. The only thing that taking care of the future does is put you in a position where you can work effectively in the now; perhaps in this way you can create the future. But you can't create the future in the future from now, and the same goes for the past. You can only change that part of the past that you can deal with in the present.

"Now that's an extremely relieving thing," I said to myself. The only part of the past that I have to deal with is that part of the past that I can handle right now.

Speaking of his own past, he said, that when you let go of the past, it lets go of you. He added that his own past used to have him, but by taking responsibility for his past he got to get his past. "Now I got a past and it aint got me." The only part of the past that exerts an influence in the present is that part of the past that is in the present, and you can deal with that right now. And what he was really saying was lighten up!

          clapclapclapclapclapclapclapclapclap
             clapclapclapclapclapclap
                     clapclap
                            Laughter!

The celebration continued with Werner introducing his parents, with whom he claims to have an "incredible relationship." He said he was clear that all the good things he had in life—from knowing what it meant to be committed to people, to being open to them, loving them—came out of his relationship to his parents. The rest, the bad part, he put together. And in return for having given him all the things in his life that are worthwhile, his parents (both est graduates) supported him by having their lives work—not by *working* at making their lives work, but by experiencing themselves as whole, complete human beings.

Werner introduced his parents.

clapclapclapclapclapclapclapclapclapclap
clapclapclapclapclapclapclap
clapclapclapclap
clapclap

It was through Werner's acknowledgment of his parents that I experienced knowing him in as much as it is possible to know a person whom you have never actually met; I say this because several months prior to the event I had also begun to realize that it was out of my relationship with my parents that I had received all the worthwhile things in my life; the rest I too had "put together." In completing my relationship with my parents, I had created the space to complete all the other relationships.

Werner introduced his children, and his ex-wife, Pat Campbell, who is now a member of the est staff; "I respect you, I admire you," he said to each one of them.

clapclapclapclapclapclapclapclapclap
clapclapclapclapclapclap
clapclapclap
clap

The last relationship he wanted to share with us was the relationship with his wife, Ellen. A great deal of Making Relationships Work came out of the experiences he and Ellen had in making their relationship work—through a long series of ups and downs. They managed to transform the quality of their relationship so that when it went up and when it went down, no matter where it was, it continued to be satisfying. The most important thing about their relationship is that it works: it presents the possibility of being able to take a relationship from wherever it is and bring it to the level in which it is absolutely and truly complete. A relationship doesn't have to be based on need, or insufficiency, or expectation. It took Ellen and him a very long time not to make it, he said, and a very short time to make it. He presented his wife Ellen.

clapclapclapclapclapclapclapclapclapclaplap
clapclapclapclapclapclapclapclap
clapclapclap

Werner read a quotation from the Bible: "A prophet is not without honor save in his own house." To have made it in his own home, with his own family, he said, was an undescribable "joy, honor, and privilege."

clapclapclapclapclapclapclapclapclap
clapclapclaplclapclap
clapclapclap

I thought of my wife, my children, and my parents, and what joy, honor, and privilege it was to have made it in *my* own home and in *my* own family. And it was an acknowledgment of the space that Werner was creating in the event that I was able to get in touch with the cumulative satisfactions that I was experiencing in all these relationships as if that experience of satisfaction were occurring in a single moment of time in which there was no past and no future. I was also able to see Werner's whole purpose in Making Relationships Work; to share his experience of his relationships working the same way he had shared his experience of his life working by creating the training. And again it was out of that shared experience that I could now say that my relationships were working, and that there was nothing I needed to do to make them work. In short, I had "gotten it," and my mind, without any of its considerations to get in the way, blew out like a candle in the wind, and I experienced loving Werner Erhard, not as the source of est or the founder of est, but as another human being.

As if reading my thoughts, he talked of being loved, absolutely and totally. It doesn't take more than one person to create that experience, and once you have truly been loved, you are able to experience it with everyone you meet.

We ended the same way we started the event, with a process, and it was in this process that Werner gave everyone in the room the opportunity to be complete in at least one relationship. He told us to take a look and see exactly where we were at in a relationship, right now!

A minute or so passed and when I was clear on where I was at in a relationship "right now," I could feel the spirit rising in that relationship, up, up, as high as I could get it.

Keep letting it go higher, said an inner voice,
    and higher,
        there's infinite space ...
            Let the spirit rise ...

Chapter IX

"I AM MOVED BY YOUR SUPPORT"

"I don't know who Werner Erhard is. I don't know what his intentions are, and I don't know what his purpose is ultimately."

—STEWART EMERY,
first est trainer

The hallway of the Civic Center stretches for about three hundred feet and is as wide as a two-lane highway; it lacks only the whizzzz of passing motor cars, and guard boxes in the breakdown lanes, to give it that lived-in look. I was waiting in the neon light with about twenty other people from New York and Boston, the way B'nai Brith volunteers or local chapter presidents of the United Fund might wait for an audience with Ted Kennedy in the Senate chambers. Brendan Hart, my trainer, walked by smiling his all-star twelve-letter-man smile and watching his son Eden toddle down the hallway. Standing next to me was Manuel Manga, master of the imagination, and Al Valentine, one of my advertising men from the *East West Journal*. At the head of the line was Lew Epstein, the onetime salesman of Israeli bonds. "Robert," he said, "if you're a good boy, you're going to get to see Werner. Isn't it exciting?"

"Sure, Lew, sure." I was as excited as he was.

Rich Aikman, who had acted as special consultant in Making Relationships Work, approached the line with his barrellike chest encased in a sleeveless blue sweater.

"Hello, New York," he said, like an amiable scout leader. "In a minute or two we're going to march down the hall and go into the party."

"Is Werner there yet?" asked Sharon Bunell, with stars in her eyes.

"Not yet," Rich said. "You can bear it, can't you?"

And there was Pat Woodell, head of enrollments. I broke out of the line and introduced myself to her; Pat looks and talks like Bess Myerson. I had intended to write the last chapter of my book on the *reasons* people give for taking or not taking the training. "Need a reason?" Pat had said at a Special Guest Seminar in Boston. "Come see me." I had planned on doing that while I was in California, but I was given a nix on the interview. "Nice meeting you," she said.

"OK, New York," Rich shouted, not acknowledging the Bostonians in the crowd. "Stay in line and proceed this way."

Column ho! We marched about two hundred feet down the granite-walled hall; Lew had dropped behind to talk to someone and I was now first in line. I showed my invitation—"I am moved by your support"—to the chic tickettaker at the entrance to Polk Hall.

"OK, come on in and have a good time," she said.

Polk Hall is about the size of a basketball court, a stone-cold tribute to the man who brought California into the Union. "Who is James K. Polk?" the Whigs used to ask. "And who were these hundred or so people in the hall?"

"Est Central." They are Werner Erhard's tried and true employees, the people who are closest to Werner's space on the organizational spiral. The men are all wearing variations of the "trainer look," trim and taut right down to where their Saks Fifth Avenue body shirts meet their tailored pants. The women are light, elegant, and bubbly, trained to carry themselves just so. Their style is similar to that of their male counterparts, with modest adaptations. Many of them are wearing pantsuits and open-neck tailored blouses, with an occasional necklace or scarf to add a touch of studied femininity.

It is like being in the center of an electric plant, and all of us are waiting for someone to turn up the juice.

Buzzzzz! A lot of potential energy was circulating around the bandstand, where a group named "White Eyes" was setting up to play acetylene rock. (Acetylene is a starting material used in the synthesis of organic compounds.) I walked toward the bandstand, which was located in the back of the room, and stood next to a refreshment table. It was spread with a paper tablecloth and plastic champagne glasses. Bomp! the sound of an electric bass cut through the underbrush of voices; the band began with a slow blues, and look! there was the steel-gray hair of Rod Logan (my second trainer) whose wiry body was now pressed against that of a woman in a flowered dress. I waved hello as they started dancing.

In the front of the room there was another refreshment table, and behind it were three black waitresses in white rayon aprons. In case anyone was hungry—though no one seemed to be—there were three huge bakery boxes with chocolate, honeydew, coconut, and plain donuts lined up like beads in an abacus. I slid toward the center of the room, still riding high on the event.

I felt the rhythm of the music as I walked. "Hey, man," Manuel said in his Spanish accent, "have some champagne." I picked up a glass and relaxed into the party; things were beginning to move along.

"Hi, how arrre you?" Her arms wrapped around me and we embraced like two samba dancers—united in body, heads far enough apart to leave room for our eyes to meet.

It was Claire Campbell, Werner Erhard's eighteen-year-old daughter; interesting that Werner should have a daughter whose name means "clear." I had met Claire in New York. She has a high-pitched sensuality and warmth about her that immediately contacts you on the level of your *being*; that is what makes her so irresistible.

"Gotta go now," she said, as she released me back into the party, and I stepped back to the table to pick up another glass of champagne. I looked toward the center of the room and saw Laurel Shief—Werner's original chief executive and the first woman to become an est trainer—dancing in the center of a circle of people. She is tough and fiery. I admired her tight peacock-blue pantsuit and wondered what she would look like without it. "Bomp, bomp, bomp," the bass pulsated.

Standing next to me on my right was Mrs. Rosenberg, Werner's mother; she was wearing a simple black dress, and even with her back turned, I could sense her vitality; she is the kind of woman who not only knows what she wants, but also knows how to get it. Werner has been called a twentieth-century samurai, and it is obvious that he inherited the sword of his intention from her.

"I can feel you behind me," she said as she turned.

I was thrilled when she introduced herself to me. A wise man once told me that if you really want to see what a man is like, pay a visit to his mother. "Were you nervous up there today?" I asked.

She looked at me as if the question were absurd. "You gotta be kidding," she says. "I was totally on purpose!"

I was struck by her use of est lingo; she was able to bring it off like a trainer in the training room. Put a pair of epaulets on her and she could have played the part of one.

"Hi, mom."

"Excuse me, will you?" Mrs. Rosenberg turned to Harry Rosenberg, Werner's younger brother. Harry, the head of est Central's graduate division, is a Bobby Kennedy prototype, and during the event Werner announced, "Harry has accepted a transfer into the office of Werner Erhard to act as my special assistant." Harry doesn't look like Werner, but you would need an electronic voice separator to tell their voices apart. He put his arms around his mother and gave her a stagy kiss, and they strolled off toward the bandstand together, leaving Werner's father, whom I had not recognized until now.

He turned toward the table, smiling congenially. Although he was wearing a dark suit, I could very easily imagine him in a butcher's apron. Mr. Rosenberg owns and operates a delicatessen outside Philadelphia. "Having a good time?" I asked him.

"Oh, yeah," he said, as if I were a long-time customer. "We always do when we're out here." He is extremely open, in a kindhearted way. I could see why Werner said that he was the man who had taught him how to love people.

"Been here a while?"

"We got in the other night and we're leaving tomorrow," he said. "Gotta get back to work, you know."

"I understand you own a restaurant in Philadelphia."

"Well, right outside it," he said, correcting me. "Ever get down to the area?"

"Not very often."

"Well, if you ever do . . ." He turned and looked at me with a twinkle in his eyes. Mr. Rosenberg is the kind of person who serves you homespun philosophy with your coffee.

"I'll bet you were proud of Werner today," I said.

"I'm more proud of the little one," said Grandpa, looking off toward the bandstand, where Werner's seven-year-old son was dancing the Hustle. "I love that kid."

Roxanne Curtis of the est public information office appeared, sashayed up to Mr. Rosenberg, and smiled "appropriately." She was wearing the "kimono look," in the latest Chinese print. Sidestepping Mr. Rosenberg, as if he had vanished into thin air, she lowered her voice and said, "Robert, I'd like to talk to you. Please come with me."

"Hi, Roxanne. Great party, isn't it?"

She pirouetted and stalked off in short strides, with her gauzy tunic wagging behind her above her broken steps. I looked down on her—she is half a head shorter than I— and I had to hold back my own stride to keep from tripping over her little feet.

Roxanne was heading for the exit. As she walked through the door, she turned like a skater cutting ice coming out of a spin, and said, "*What* were you *doing* talking to *Werner's* mother and father?" She was trembling with anger and anxiety, and her eyes bulged with emotion as she waited for my reply. "Well—?"

I was taken aback; only a few hours ago, I had seen Roxanne and swept her off her feet with a big hug. "I was standing by the refreshment table and Werner's mother turned around to talk to me. I wasn't interviewing her, and I didn't ask her any questions pertaining to Werner or est."

What could be ticking her off?

"I don't want to talk about it. I *don't* want to talk about it," she said, straightening her tunic. Roxanne seemed to be more aware of her appearance than she was of herself.

"Then why did you call me out here?"

"I don't want to talk about it," she said again. "And as far as the interviews are concerned, that's out! It may change next week or the week after, but right now, they're out, and I want you to 'get' that—and if you say 'I get it *but*—'"

I was beginning to catch on: Roxanne was hooked on what she thought my reactions would be to not getting an interview with Werner. At this point, it made absolutely no difference to me. I had completed my relationship with Werner at the event; my book was already written. "Roxanne, I don't need an interview with Werner or with anyone else; it's complete for me."

"I don't want to talk about it. Maybe Monday I will," she said with bureaucratic authority.

"OK, great. I'm going back into the party now," I said calmly.

"Look at the space you're in— Look at the space you're in," she stammered. "I think you ought to go home," she said, looking at me as if a wart had suddenly appeared on the tip of my nose. "Look at the space you're in. . . ."

As I gazed into Roxanne's cold-blue, alabaster eyes, the veil of estian sophistication parted and beneath it I could see her years of struggle to stay in control.

"I'm going back into the party now."

"Wait! You ought to look at the space you're in."

It was only minutes after the event. "I am in one of the highest spaces I have ever been in."

"I don't get a lot of that from you—" she said.

I didn't know what language Roxanne was speaking, but it wasn't English.

"Roxanne, what is it that you want to tell me?"

I had interrupted her. "Will you just let me finish what I'm saying?" she yelped in a huff.

"Roxanne!"

"Shut up! Shut up!" I couldn't believe what I was hearing; I stared at her in amazement: Her chicly coiffed blonde ringlets seemed a little limp.

Standing next to Roxanne now was a guy named Will Webber, an est heavy, the man Werner hired to "create a perfect organization." With his hand cupped around his chin, he looked like a cross between the wrestler Bruno San Martino and Rodin's "Le Penseur." Will was listening attentively.

"He won't let me finish a sentence," she said to Will, looking for approval. Will didn't budge.

"Go ahead," I said, and apologized for interrupting her. "I guess I still don't have any idea what you are trying to tell me."

Roxanne was at a loss for words; she sputtered out another blizzard of est terminology, and petered out.

"OK, now that you've said what you've said, all I want to tell you is that I have done nothing inappropriate at this party, and—"

"Shut up," she repeated. "I'm not only talking about tonight."

"What are you talking about? Be specific."

"Well one thing you did was write Pat Woodell a memo asking to interview her."

"That's accurate," I said, "and I sent you a copy of that memo knowing that the interview was subject to your approval."

"A memo," she said indignantly, throwing up her hands. "A copy!"

Will was still rubbing his chin.

I was a little embarrassed. I didn't want Will to get the wrong impression of my relationship with Roxanne, so I told him that we had had a very good relationship, that we really liked each other, that Roxanne had visited me in my home, and that up to this point we had never squabbled.

Roxanne said, "Sometimes I worry about him too much."

It seemed as if she was about to cool off and I thought that the best thing I could do to assist her was to give her her space. "I'm going back into the party now," I said.

"I want you to get the way things work around here," she muttered again, looking to Will again for approval.

I walked back into the party, thinking that in many cases, Roxanne would be the only person in the est organization whom the public would ever meet. It was her job as manager of the public information office to make initial contacts with the media, and it seemed to me that she would somehow have to learn to personify the things that Werner Erhard and the est organization were supposed to represent. Well, maybe she was having a hard night; letting these thoughts be, I reentered the atmosphere of the party.

Al Valentine swung past me, shimmying through an updated version of the twist. "Hey, Robert," he asked gaily, "why aren't you dancing?"

I thanked him for the suggestion and began looking

around for Claire Campbell. I had been back at the party approximately seven minutes when Roxanne appeared again; she seemed to have regained her composure. I was about to ask her to dance, when she said,

"Will wants to talk to you."

"OK, tell him I'm over here."

"He wants you to come to him," she said coyly.

"OK. Where is he?"

"Well, he was right over here a minute ago," she said.

I looked around for him, but as I turned toward the wall, I saw Gerry Goodman; Gerry was standing there holding his notebook of clever witticisms and his act together.

Known in the "agreement" as "Adam Smith," author of *The Money Game* and *Powers of the Mind*, Gerry had recently winged his way through an article about est in *New York* magazine without once making personal contact with its actual substance. In *Powers of the Mind*, he had shown himself to be a gourmand of the "consciousness circuit," having swallowed it up like a box of assorted bonbons.

I walked over to introduce myself to Gerry; and as I was about to call his attention away from his notebook, Roxanne tugged at my elbow and said, "Where do you think you're going?"

"I'm going to talk to Gerry," I said. "I can talk to Gerry." After all, he wasn't a member of the group of people that Roxanne had referred to as "the family."

Roxanne slipped in between Gerry and me, keeping one eye on me and the other on his notebook.

Gerry stepped to the side and offered the notebook for her approval. What innocence! Roxanne looked at him in much the same way a second-grade teacher would look at someone whom she has caught drawing pictures of wedding-cake battleships in a notebook intended for the intricacies of the Palmer method.

Will Webber pranced up to me like a strutting bull and then stopped two or three steps away, with his toes forward and his shoulders back. He is big and meaty, 180 pounds of pure protein, water, and hydrogenated fats; but the talisman that lies against the thick bed of black hair on his chest acts as a tenderizer of sorts.

I met him on an equal plane of certainty; his eyes have a pensive quality that seems to balance the massive head in which they are set; he is not insensitive. But what did he want to talk to me about?

It took him about thirty seconds to decide. "It's time for you to leave," he said, as if he were offering me a chocolate mint.

"What?" I couldn't believe what I was hearing.

"C'mon," he said with sullen composure.

Nor could I understand what I had done to create this situation. I had come to the party without any intention of writing about it. "I want you to tell me why you are asking me to leave," I said.

"I'm not going to tell you why," he said. "It's time for you to go."

I looked at the corners of his mouth to see if they would reveal a lack of conviction behind his words, but they were stone solid—no emotion. "Will, I have a personal invitation from Werner to be at this party. I haven't said or done anything inappropriate, and unless you can demonstrate that I have, I intend to stay."

"I know," he said with a suave sophistication in his swelling voice. "You're the innocent victim of circumstances."

I let it go by—this ultimate est put-down, this disemboweler of all the "mechanical assholes" that had taken the training, this imploder of resistance, this breaker of minds, this can opener of hardened hearts, this atomic-ray gunshot that could reduce a person to a few shriveled-up molecules with a single laser-like blast and leave an impression of his body on the nearest wall. "Why are you asking me to leave? Why did you invite me here in the first place?"

I was perplexed.

Will leaned back looking for something "appropriate" to say. "Look," he said, "you've been disinvited." How totally appropriate! And then, with added certainty: "you've been disinvited, that's all."

Will was intelligent, but this was too much; it was the kind of answer Ron Ziegler used to give the White House press corps. "Who gave the order to disinvite me?" I asked.

Will leaned back again to think. He couldn't incriminate Werner; besides, at this point Werner wasn't even in the room. Leaning forward he said, "Don disinvited you." (As if he were offering me a cup of café au lait to go with the after-dinner mint.) Don Cox, the president and chief executive officer of est.

"I want to hear that from Don."

Roxanne cut in, "Well, just the fact that you're not leaving shows that you don't respect Werner and Don." Will looked at Roxanne in agreement.

Don Cox had made his way to est from dissolving people's teeth and intestines as president of the Coca Cola Bottling Company of California; I respected him for it because in this way he had helped to give the natural foods movement a *raison d'être*. I also respected Don because he had changed his occupation, but I wondered if he was part of that new breed of corporate managers that was trying to surround the new culture with sophisticated management techniques. Whereas Werner always signed his letters, "Love, Werner," Don signed his, "Warm regards, Don." He was a cool corporation executive but at least he was now in the business of serving other people.

Our conversation went on like this a while longer, until Will lost his steady stare and started to blink.

"C'mon," Will gesticulated, pushing a hand against my chest—not enough pressure for me to make something out of it, but an implicit suggestion, that if I didn't move willingly, he was prepared to throw me out bodily.

I looked at the gathering reinforcements behind him. Roxanne was standing there, smiling like a shark, waiting to see what would happen. I wasn't going to mess around with that kind of "agreement"; reality, being physical, was obviously on Will's side. I was also beginning to feel as if a Saturday night barroom brawl was about to take place. "OK," I said, "I'm going to walk over there and pick up my jacket, and then I'll move out to the hallway where we can continue this discussion."

Will agreed, and watched me closely with his radar eyes as I walked to the back of Polk Hall to pick up my coat. Leaving the room, I saw Werner entering from another room on the opposite side. I was certain that he had no idea of what was going on or of the implications of this abuse of power—and that was precisely the point. How much of what was going on in the est organization did he actually know about?

Roxanne followed us out to the hallway, but walked away as soon as Will and I resumed our conversation. She returned a minute or two later with a bottle of champagne in one hand, and a steamed Oscar Mayer hot dog in the other. "I really don't have anything more to say to you," she said, sinking her teeth into the bright yellow mustard. "Besides"—she did a perfect Jean Harlow turn that sent her tunic up in the air with a flutter—"I'm hostessing this party." And she sashayed off.

Will and I began to ease up on each other as the tension we were both experiencing began to change into its opposite. I heard a voice in the auditorium shout, *"Werner Erhard, why are you so fucking right?"* It was followed by Werner's self-amused giggle. What exquisite self-control! The man was a true knight.

The question reminded me of one I had dropped forever during the event, only to have it reappear now. I had been told that Werner had a "powerful relationship" with everyone in the est organization, one in which there is "an agreed-upon power source and the people who feed that power never get to make the power source wrong." Did this mean that Werner always got to be right? I wasn't so concerned with Werner's being right as I was with the idea that the powerful relationships in the est organization proceeded from sergeant to corporal to the buck privates in the "assistant's program"—all the way down the dogshit chain of command. What were the possibilities of the top sergeants and corporals using their power unethically? "Get the job done and I don't care what you have to do to get it done," I had heard one staff member say to a group of assistants. And to what lengths would these people go in order to "produce the results?" After all, they had an "agreement!"

And if Werner and his honchos always had to be right, was it wrong, then, to dissent? I had seen one seminar leader crumple up in total bewilderment when he was asked to criticize est for two minutes. Was I considered a dissenter of some kind, a threat to the established order of things?

A circle of people emerged from Polk Hall, about a dozen of them; they looked as if they were clinging to a life raft. I could barely see Werner's head in the center of that circle, but as he moved toward the side exit of the auditorium, they heeled to his every step. How similar these people looked to those I had seen clinging to the saffron robes of Swami Satchidananda and the white dashiki of Yogi Bajan, a year earlier at Kohoutek.

"Let's go," Will said. "Out!"

"Wait a minute," I said. "I'd really like to meet Werner."

Will walked over to the crowd and poked his head into the circle. A huge black bouffant hairdo turned out of the swarm. There was a mass of stop-sign-red lipstick daubed across the woman's mouth. Her head began to describe slow figure eights in the air, and the two halves of the stop sign silently opened and closed around the word, "NO." God save the king from the love of the people. "We got to get him out of here," said Werner's personal valet, Jack Rafferty, ex-nightclub owner, as he hurried Werner along to the waiting limousine outside. Werner took a step or two and the circle of electrons spiraled around him.

Was Werner merely hiding in the center of that circle? I recalled a quote from the newsletter put out by Swami Muktananda's people. (Est had sponsored Muktananda's recent tour of the US.) "Sitting on my right is Sri Yogi Werner," Swami said. "I call him that not because he calls himself that, but because I can see where he's at. I have only one question to ask him: Why does he hide himself so much? What is the big secret?"

And the words of Lao-tsu came to mind as a summation: "So as ever hidden, we should look at its inner essence. As always manifest, we should look at its outer aspects."

Will, getting impatient, gripped his heavy hand around the back of my neck, and said, "Move on!" There was no violence in the gesture, but the force was again implied.

"I'm ready to go!" I pulled out of Will's grasp to face him one last time. "I have a lot of questions about est, Will, that no one will answer."

He told me that I would have to go through "channels," and the only channels I could go through were Roxanne Curtis and Arthur Crowley of J. D. Bettelbaum in New York.

The last time I had talked to Arthur Crowley, he said he was "fucking irritated with the est organization," and added "I don't care if you tell them so!" I told Will.

"So you better have Roto-Rooter come and clean out your channels, Will."

He laughed.

"Anyway, thanks a lot." I meant it sincerely, "I've gotten a lot out of this, more than I ever expected!"

We shook hands and I left the party.

* * *

My immediate intention was to call Paul Hawken, whom I would be staying with in San Anselmo. It would take him about an hour to come down and pick me up at the Civic, he said, so I sat down in an alcove leading to the balcony. The doors of the building were open and there was a chill wind blowing into the dank hallway. "What hypocrisy!" I muttered as someone walked by carrying a sign with the est logo on it, the orchid leaves. (In Chinese art, the orchid is a symbol of love, beauty, elegance, and the perfect human being.) Seek beauty and it shall become ugliness, I said to myself, thinking back to the party. Seek elegance and it shall become a mere trapping. Seek perfection and it shall become self-righteousness. I laughed aloud, and leaning back against the granite wall, I closed my eyes. I hadn't slept in over thirty hours, but I had no intention of going to sleep in this cement stairwell, to which only a few hours ago I had descended with so much affinity and affection for Werner Erhard and the est organization. What a paradox! But *"C'est la vie."* Everything changes into its opposite. I got up to go outside for a walk, maybe a cup of tea.

I had been told in est never to deny my own experience, and what my experience told me was that I still had a great many unanswered questions about the source of the est universe, and the organization that had treated me and other people like so many straw dogs. I could no longer deny these questions, nor could I "process them out" as I had in the past; with each step I took they were flashing on and off like a thousand neon lights in the darkness.

It was after hours and the streets were empty. Rounding the corner of Polk Street, I looked up at the radiance of the moon. Had it not been for the curiosity of science, one would never know it had a dark side. It seemed the same with the est organization; its light was so strong that one would never know it, too, had a dark side. One would remain ignorant of the realities of est, if his curiosity did not lead him to see the organization as a whole. Going into the training, it was as if I had been given a pair of emerald-green spectacles that allowed me to see est only as a perfect representation of the highest principles of humanity. But now that I was launched into my space, and no longer holding back my questions about est, I could perceive—even with my eyes closed—something that went beyond the shining silver mountains and the rocky craters revealed by the reflected light. I was beginning to see the part of the est organization that was hidden in darkness— the part of Werner Erhard that one had to go behind the scenes to observe.

It took Western science thousands of years and millions of dollars worth of technology to show us what the dark side of the moon looked like, but it had taken only four months and the incident at Polk Hall for me to catch a telescopic glimpse of the side of est that faced the black shimmer of space. What a fool I had been! What a muddled mind I had, to have looked upon my extrication from the party as a misfortune! It was not a matter of coincidence that I had been asked to leave, I thought. "There are no accidents in the universe." It had taken the incident in Polk Hall to wake me up to my responsibility to ask my questions.

I continued walking until I came upon the dimly lit entrance of the Bumble Bee restaurant. As I opened the door a bell rang inside my head: I would have to ask my questions in a way that didn't make them seem like conclusions. (The only conclusion I could form right now was that no one in the est organization would answer the questions.) I ordered a cup of tea and began a dialogue of opposites with my mind that ended up with, "Go ahead, ask your goddamn questions."

"Cream or lemon?" the waitress asked. She was standing in front of me with a chartreuse enamel pot filled with hot tea.

I looked at her Botticelli belly as if I were looking at Venus on the half shell, and said, "Lemon."

Sipping my tea, I began writing down my questions while keeping a wandering eye on the waitress. I have a passion for waitresses. It is their occupational purpose to "serve other people" and like the people in the est organization, they do it with various degrees of intention. How many times had I gone to the best restaurants in search of masters of the serving tray, only to have a hefty waitress throw my plate of victuals on the table like a ceramic frisbee. "Eat this!" Was the est organization really serving people, or was it merely serving its own self-image? "We're the biggest and best around," I had heard a trainer say. "Our purpose is to serve Werner." Got it. And was Werner really serving people, and to what end? "That's for openers," I said to myself, as I completed a short list of questions.

"Would you like your check now?" Venus asked.

"Sure," I said, and as I reached into my pocket, I pulled out the telephone number of Stewart Emery, the ex-est first trainer who had left Werner Erhard in the spring of 1975 after three years of active duty to start something called "Actualizations."

"What the hell!" I paid my check and went to the back of the restaurant to call Stewart in Los Angeles. I didn't know whether he would talk to me or not. Alexander Everett, whom I had called the previous day to see what Werner Erhard had taken from Mind Dynamics, had told me that Werner had invited him to a special meeting and asked him to make an agreement not to talk to the media. Had someone spoken to Stewart, too?

"Hello, this is Stewart Emery."

I was immediately concerned with establishing a rapport with Stewart. After my dealings with est I was beginning to think I had the plague. So I communicated to him that I was not out to get est, and that I would not use what he said out of context. I told him that I had been the editor of the *East West Journal*, and that I was now writing a book about est, and that the est organization was totally unwilling to communicate with me.

"Go ahead," he said, "ask your questions. I will not lie to you; I will tell you the truth. If I don't want to answer I will tell you that I prefer not to. If I don't know the answers, I will tell you I don't know them. But you can be certain when you put the phone down that whatever I've told you is true."

Stewart spoke in an Australian accent, and his voice was as clear as a bell, ringing with overtones. I asked Stewart if he had been contacted by anyone on the est staff and asked to make an agreement not to talk to the media about his experiences with Werner Erhard and est. He answered that, like Alexander, he had been called and asked to make such an agreement. (Both Stewart and Werner were Mind Dynamics instructors; that is how they met.) He also said that he had told Don Cox (the person who had contacted him) that he was unwilling to make that agreement. I was interested in Stewart's answer. It presented some intriguing possibilities about the est organization: Specifically, when you control information and deny access to it by the media, when you have one man at the top of an organization whose position is inviolable, and when the people in that organization will do anything that isn't blatantly illegal "to produce results," you have all the elements of a totalitarian state.

Stewart was later quoted in the *East West Journal* as saying that he had been at meetings where ". . . Werner openly told people that if they were working for him they had no rights, no privileges. They were not to have any desires or intentions of their own; they were not to foster any relationships for their own purposes." And they were to do only what "served Werner."

"Who is Werner Erhard?" I asked him about the quotation from Swami Muktananda—"What's the big secret?"

He didn't understand the question at first, saying that it had always been Werner's policy to keep a low profile with the media. When I reminded Stewart that Swami Muktananda had spent a great deal of time with Werner— and had come up with the same question that I had come up with without ever having met Werner—Stewart replied, "My experience has been that I can't say I know Werner Erhard, and I too have spent time with him."

"One of the things that's occurred to me, Stewart, is that Werner created the est organization as a protective covering, an iron curtain for him to hide behind. Now I talked to Mike Murphy, the founder of the Esalen Institute, about this, and he said that he wouldn't buy it; he said the guy's a complete extrovert. What really concerns me, with all those people giving up their rights to 'serve Werner,' is Werner's purpose. What is it?"

"That I don't know the answer to," Stewart said. "There are some questions that I couldn't answer in my three years there, and that's one of them. I do not know what Werner Erhard's intentions are, or why he created est. I have no idea why he put it together, or what his purpose is, and ultimately I don't know where he's at about it all, personally. I haven't known that for the last couple of years, and that's exactly where I'm at about it—I don't know."

I was surprised by Stewart's answer. With so much "agreement" on Werner's purpose "to serve other people" I thought it had been a little bit farfetched for me even to have asked the question. But again, without much evidence to doubt Werner, and no personal contact with him, I had come up with the same kind of question that Stewart had come up with as a member of the inner circle. Maybe we were both crazy, but all this raised the question of whether Werner was using his power responsibly. I wasn't so concerned with the possibility that Werner might abuse his power as I was with the possibility that he might lose touch with it as it was channeled down into the power pockets of the organization. I had overlooked the "arm-bending" telephone tactics I had seen the people in the est organization use, as it seemed a relatively harmless way of getting people into the training; but on a larger scale those tactics might be dangerous. When power is used with understanding and compassion it can serve to preserve the integrity of something, but without that understanding and compassion, it becomes abusive. Giving

Werner the benefit of the doubt, how persevering was he in monitoring the possible abuse of power within his own rapidly expanding organization? And to what extent was he the "source" of the behavior I had seen demonstrated in Polk Hall?

"I see what you see going on," Stewart said, "and that's my criticism of the est organization. I think the source of it is wherever Werner's coming from, and I don't know where that is. I have never seen him act publicly the way some of his people do, but I know that they are the way they are—so it can only be that they are dramatizing their own sense of where he's coming from. And since he allows this to exist, he's got to be responsible for it—"

I had heard about four different accounts of why Stewart left the est organization, so I asked him his reasons; and he said that he had gotten to the point where he wanted to express himself independently of Werner's point of view. As for the specific circumstances, Stewart and another est employee, Carol Augustus, took a weekend holiday in March of 1975 to visit a man named Peter Wagner, who at one time had been considered the Chief Executive Officer of est. Wagner had gotten together with an ex-est researcher for the purpose of producing something they called an "entertainment"; his notion was to concoct a twelve-hour condensation of the est training with multimedia effects. Wagner asked Stewart if he wanted "in" and Stewart said that he would certainly be willing to take a further look at the project when it was complete. Apparently, Werner's office knew that Stewart was having conversations with Peter Wagner; and later that month, when Stewart was in Washington, DC, about to do a pre-training, he got a phone call from Don Cox. Stewart's account of that phone call was reported in the *East West Journal*.

"Stewart," Cox said, "I understand that you saw Peter Wagner." I said, "That is exactly what I did." And he said, "I understand that Carol was also there." I said,

"That's accurate." He said, "I understand that you looked at a program that Peter Wagner's putting together." I said, "Yes, that is accurate." And he said, "Did you send a memo through to Werner's office or to my office that you were going to see Peter Wagner?" I said, "No, it was my annual vacation and I got three days off, so I went down there, and Werner's office is aware of my relationship with Peter." And he said, "Well, I consider your presence there and Carol's presence there to be a disservice to Werner. It indicates that we can't trust you. And that's also true of Carol. So my response to that is I have terminated Carol, and asked her to leave the premises. Now what we have to discuss is the continuation of your relationship to est. I would be willing for you to be at est only if I were absolutely certain that you had given up all your own intentions, purposes, desires, and objectives in life, and had only those . . . that Werner agreed for you to have. I'd like to know where you are about that?" I said, "Don, you just at this moment represent to me everything about the est organization that I think is unworkable. That's all I have time to be with at this point. I have two hundred and fifty people waiting downstairs who expect me to make them excited about the est training and the est organization, and since I'm a professional, I will go down there and get my job done."

I asked Stewart if the things we talked about earlier, concerning the dramatization of where some of Werner's people thought he was coming from, originated in the marine-boot-camp, Kaiser-Wilhelm, General-George-Patton atmosphere of the training. Even within myself, I had witnessed the tendency to glamorize and emulate the trainer's power, and it was precisely that attraction, that glamorization that seemed to bring so many people back into the organization to assist. Would the marine-boot-camp tactics and game plans used in the training seep out into the world, the same way they had seeped into the organization?

Werner was talking about having forty million graduates in the US alone, and it was rumored that Werner might some day want to run for president. Discounting that rumor, what impact would all this have on the democratic values of a free society? What impact would it have on civil liberties? What impact would it have on everyone's right to life, liberty, and the pursuit of happiness in the manner of his own choice?

These were not easy questions to answer, but they were important questions to ask. "It's all right not to have answers," Stewart said, "as long as we don't stop asking the questions. I have a particular theory about life—that by the time you get all the answers, all the questions have changed. What's important is that you ask the questions, rather than just accepting the answers that you want to believe are true."

Stewart and I completed our conversation by sharing the value that we both had gotten out of our association with Werner and est. "I love Werner totally," he said, "and I think that he has made an enormous contribution to the lives of many people, including my own."

I told Stewart that I supported Werner and that the best way I could do that was to ask my questions.

Stewart was off to catch a plane, and I had to get back to the Civic Center to catch my ride. On the way back, I considered my conversation with Stewart, and I knew— I knew so clearly—that only one person in the world was more of a totalitarian than Werner Erhard, and that person was me. I would have set up my organization in exactly the same way that he set up his; and I would have avoided answering people's questions to the same extent that Werner avoids answering them. I would have hidden to the same extent that Werner may be hiding, and I would have had people like Don Cox and Will Webber doing the same jobs they were being paid to do and with the same excellence. I looked back over my whole experience with est, and I could say with certainty that the training had been of incredible value to me, that the seminar program had been of incredible value to me, and that every est event I had ever attended had been of incredible value to me.

I had only one question left in my mind, and that was this: Was est working for other people to the extent that it was working for me? I didn't have any idea whether the training had worked for six other people or sixty-five thousand; and to tell people after they completed the training that they had "got it," that they were now "enlightened," seemed as patently ridiculous as Kohoutek. As Stewart had said, "There's an 'it' to 'get' every minute of every day, and the extent to which you've 'got it'—or not—depends on the extent to which you are 'getting it' every minute of every day."

I looked up at the moon, but now, instead of thinking of what was behind it, I saw that it was complete in its radiance. I also saw that it didn't make any difference that the moon had a dark side. The only way it could have a light side was by having a dark side. It was the same with Werner Erhard and the est organization. "It's all perfect the way it is," I thought.

Reaching the steps of the Civic Center, I recalled the last time I had left this building, following the Kohoutek celebration in 1974. I had come to Kohoutek in search, and I had left in search, but I was now leaving in certainty; and somehow it had taken Werner Erhard and the est organization to show me that a search always brings you back to where you are. I had already "gotten it"; and no longer being in a search, I was no longer in search of est; it was complete for me.

A green Volvo station wagon pulled up in front of the building; it was Paul's. I told him what had happened and we drove in relative silence past the boat yards and the trestles. It was when we passed through the toll booth at the Golden Gate Bridge—the very same place where Werner had had his "experience"—that I realized why est worked and why it didn't work, and that taking responsibility for my life worked. I gazed up at the moon, then into the dark waters of San Francisco Bay where the co-flows, cross-flows, and counter-flows all were moving with certainty into the sea. Smiling serenely, I thought of something Werner had said in the event. It was a quotation from Dag Hammarskjold: "Never, never, for the sake of peace and quiet, deny your own experience." I looked back at the party and at the hills of Marin County, and knew it was time to move on.

EPILOGUE

Two weeks after my return from California, I received a telephone call from Don Cox. He said that he was prepared to offer his support and the support of the est organization in reviewing my book for accuracy. Don also said that he would allow me to interview trainers, and possibly even Werner. I thought about Don's offer and said I would get back to him.

Several days later I received a letter from Werner Erhard, which concluded: "You have my intention for completing the project of your book in a way that allows you maximum nourishment and satisfaction for yourself, and in a way that makes the greatest possible contribution. I know that's your purpose." It was signed "I love you, Werner."

I also received a telephone call from Morty Lefkoe, the new manager of the public information office, saying that the policy toward the media had changed and that Werner had told him to make available whatever information I needed. But by this time my book was already written; trying to go back and change it would have been like trying to change the past in the past. As Werner says, "The only part of the past that you can affect is that part of it that exists in the present," and I can handle that right now. I would like to say that I stand behind Werner Erhard's good intentions, that I support his purpose unconditionally, and that I could present him to anyone and say, "This is a man who has earned my ultimate respect."

In the *Legend of Musashi*, a Samurai movie I once saw, there is a scene where two master swordsmen (who will eventually meet each other in battle), cross paths on a mountaintop. As Musashi descends into the lush green valley, his opponent turns and says, "If he develops, so will I. . . ."

I want to conclude by saying that all Werner had to do was make his life work, and three years later my life began to work. All Werner had to do was make his relationships work, and three years later my relationships began to work. As Werner develops, so will I. . . .

ACKNOWLEDGMENTS

When you've said all the good things, and all the bad things, all that is left to say is, "I love you."

Acknowledgment is the basis of all communication, and I can hardly express the acknowledgment I would like to extend to all the following people:

It was Perry Garfinkle who got me started by asking me to write an article for the *Boston Globe*; it was Suzanne Wexler, of the est staff in California, whose support enabled me to complete that article; and it was Ellis Amburn of Delacorte who provided me with the opportunity to write this book.

It was my wife Cynthia whose inspiration, support, and enthusiasm made it possible to see it through. Sandy McDonald, a professional copy editor, provided me with an invaluable service by "separating the bullshit from the gunsmoke"; while Gabriel Heilig, a raconteur and poet, acted as my minister of imagery and description. It was my mother and her IBM, however, who turned these words into typescript.

My sincerest thanks go to Werner Erhard, the source of est and much of what is in this book. I would like to acknowledge the people on the est staff for supporting Werner and for creating the space in which I experienced the training and the seminar programs. Those who I would especially like to acknowledge are Landon Carter, Ted Long, David Norris, Michael Rosenbaum, Tracy Goss, Rich Aikman, Pat Woodell, Irving Bernstein, Vince Drucker, Hal Isen, Roy Bynum, Randy McNamara, Kerry Williams, Morty Lefkoe, and Francine Epstein. I would like to thank Lew Epstein for being the friendliest person I met in the est organization, and Angelo Damelio for being the funniest. Don Cox, who called me toward the end of this writing, deserves the Alexander Graham Bell award for opening up communication.

I would like to thank all those people who shared in the est experience with me, among them Matt Chait, Claire Campbell, Dora Hawken, James Hargrove, Linda Bergquist, Keith Varnum, Janet Vohs, Manuel Manga, Anne Gorden, Sharon Magnuson, Al Valentine, Christina Twarkins, Jimmy Silver, Stephen Uprichard, and Eric and Peggy Utne. I would like to acknowledge my best friends, David Korkosz, Bruce Gardiner, and—particularly—Paul Hawken. Paul was enormously helpful to me in bringing the book to completion.

I would like to thank John Denver, Tom Wait, Yehudi Menuhin, Stephanie Grappelli, and Joni Mitchell for the inspiration of their music. Special thanks go to Antonio Vivaldi and Johann Sebastian Bach for demonstrating to me that in the Kingdom of Heaven, a movement is followed by a rest.

"You don't know how good it feels to acknowledge people...."

      clapclapclapclapclapclapclapclapclapclap
           clapclapclapclapclap
                  clap

BESTSELLERS FROM DELL

fiction

- [ ] SHOGUN by James Clavell $2.75 (7800-15)
- [ ] RICH MAN, POOR MAN by Irwin Shaw $1.95 (7424-29)
- [ ] GHOSTBOAT
  by George Simpson and Neal Burger $1.95 (5421-00)
- [ ] ODE TO BILLY JOE by Herman Raucher $1.75 (6628-17)
- [ ] WHERE ARE THE CHILDREN? by Mary H. Clark $1.95 (9593-04)
- [ ] THE GARGOYLE CONSPIRACY
  by Marvin H. Alpert $1.95 (5239-02)
- [ ] THE FORTY-FIRST THIEF
  by Edward A. Pollitz $1.75 (5420-01)
- [ ] CRY MACHO by N. Richard Nash $1.95 (4915-06)
- [ ] THE OTHER SIDE OF MIDNIGHT
  by Sidney Sheldon $1.75 (6067-07)
- [ ] MARATHON MAN by William Goldman..... $1.95 (5502-02)

non-fiction

- [ ] BREACH OF FAITH by Theodore H. White .. $1.95 (0780-14)
- [ ] GREEN BEACH by James Leasor $1.95 (4491-03)
- [ ] HOLLYWOOD BABYLON by Kenneth Anger .. $5.95 (5325-07)
- [ ] DR. SIEGAL'S NATURAL FIBER PERMANENT WEIGHT LOSS DIET
  by Sanford Siegal, D.O., M.D. $1.75 (7790-25)
- [ ] THE LAST TESTAMENT OF LUCKY LUCIANO
  by Martin A. Gosch and Richard Hammer ... $1.95 (4940-21)
- [ ] THE ULTRA SECRET by F. W. Winterbotham .. $1.95 (9061-07)
- [ ] MEETING AT POTSDAM by Charles L. Mee, Jr. $1.95 (5449-08)
- [ ] EST: Playing the Game the New Way
  by Carl Frederick $3.95 (2365-13)
- [ ] WAMPETERS, FOMA & GRANFALLOONS
  by Kurt Vonnegut, Jr. $1.95 (8533-25)
- [ ] THE NEW ASSERTIVE WOMAN by L. Z. Bloom,
  K. Coburn and J. Pearlman $1.75 (6393-10)

Buy them at your local bookstore or use this handy coupon for ordering:

Dell | **DELL BOOKS**
P.O. BOX 1000, PINEBROOK, N.J. 07058

Please send me the books I have checked above. I am enclosing $_____
(please add 35¢ per copy to cover postage and handling). Send check or money order—no cash or C.O.D.'s.

Mr/Mrs/Miss_____

Address_____

City_____State/Zip_____

---

offer expires 7/77